ARISE OUT OF THE LOCK

ARISE OUT OF THE LOCK

*50 Bangladeshi Women Poets
to Commemorate the
Golden Jubilee of Bangladesh*

Translated by **Nabina Das**
Curated by **Alam Khorshed**

BALESTIER PRESS
LONDON · SINGAPORE

Balestier Press
Centurion House, London TW18 4AX
www.balestier.com

Arise out of the Lock
Copyright © Nabina Das & Alam Khorshed, 2022

A CIP catalogue record for this book
is available from the British Library.

ISBN 978 1 913891 14 5

Cover image: Exterminating Angel, a sculpture by Novera Ahmed

All rights reserved. No part of this publication may be reproduced, stored in a retrieval system or transmitted in any form or by any means, electronic or mechanical, without the prior written permission of the publisher of this book.

CONTENTS

Dedication 5

Foreword 7

Curator's Introduction 11

Translator's Note 17

Arise out of the Lock

    Sufia Kamal 26

    Khaleda Edib Chowdhury 28

    Anwara Syed Haq 30

    Farida Majid 32

    Meherun Nesa 34

    Zeenat Ara Rafiq 37

    Suraiya Khanum 40

    Rubi Rahman 43

    Kazi Rozi 45

Zarina Akhter *47*

Shamim Azad *49*

Nasreen Naim *52*

Dilara Hafiz *54*

Anjana Saha *56*

Nurunnahar Shirin *58*

Let There Be Some Anger

Nasima Sultana *61*

Shahjadi Anzuman Ara *63*

Jharna Rahman *65*

Taslima Nasrin *68*

Rahima Akhter Kalpana *71*

Ferdous Nahar *74*

Bilora Chowdhury *77*

Shahnaz Nasreen *80*

Kochi Reza *83*

Leesa Gazi *85*

Shahnaz Munni *87*

Shelly Naz *89*

Nahar Monica *91*

Aysa Jhorna *94*

What's a Woman Gotta Do in Heaven

Shanta Maria *97*

Megh Aditi *100*

Monika Chakraborty *103*

Alaka Nandita *106*

Farhana Rahman *109*

Junan Nashit *111*

Nahida Ashrafi *114*

Audity Falguni *117*

Rahima Afrooz Munni *119*

Novera Hossain *121*

Jahanara Perveen *123*

Shakira Parvin *125*

Sabera Tabassum *129*

Asma Beethe *132*

Nitu Purna   *135*

Asma Odhora   *137*

Afroja Shoma   *140*

Rimjhim Ahmed   *143*

Shafinur Shafin   *146*

Mahi Flora   *149*

Shweta Shatabdi Esh   *151*

Poets' Bios   *153*

Curator's Bio   *169*

Translator's Bio   *170*

Glossary   *171*

Dedication

To the first female poet of Bangladesh, Chandrabati (Approx. 1550-1600) who rewrote Ramayan, the great Indian epic, from a woman's point of view depicting Sita as its protagonist

And

To honour the supreme sacrifice of the countless *Birangonas* or war heroines of 1971, whose suffering and resistance paved the way for the independence of Bangladesh

Foreword

The poems in this ambitious collection are by women poets writing in Bangla, who have emerged from the land that is now Bangladesh—having lived, or are still living here, or are now part of the first-generation diaspora.

What beautifully comes through in this thoughtfully curated and faithfully translated volume, is Bangladesh emerging as a country on its own terms, with this collage of writing from women, rooted in a rich eclectic cultural history, and yet with a contemporary and cosmopolitan sensibility.

Much has been written about the economic success and social progress of Bangladesh, especially highlighting women's empowerment. However, the creative spaces in Bangladesh, especially in poetry, have been largely dominated by men. Dipping into this book will be like the delicious potential discovery of a treasure trove of work by women who bring out varied aspects of the collective Bangladeshi experience. The poems really give a sense of what Bangladesh is, 50 years after its inception; while celebrating the rich history of people of an ancient land over millennia. Bangladesh today is an amalgamation and confluence of our pluralism, diversity and syncretism, and the energy of a young country free-er from rigid prescriptive structures, forging our own future—though still with a plethora of barriers. These come through in the work, with force and creativity, but without melodrama.

The inferences to the culture, the land and nature form the backdrop to women navigating their reality. With echoes of Rabindranath Tagore, Jibanananda Das, and Kazi Nazrul Islam, they get strength from the familiar, symbolic and concrete, to express themselves, and frame and voice their resistance. The historic influence of Islam, Hinduism, Buddhism, Animism, Tantric, and other practices, as well as the sheer potency and beauty of the fertile land and mother nature, are drawn on, interpreted and used as they see fit.

Fearless, confident, defying expectations, and covering age-old emotions like anger, love, and dissonance with the status quo, many of the poems display a boldness of material and direction that is able to capture the essence of what could represent the modern Bangladeshi women.

Whether it's the pioneering force of Sufia Kamal, the seasoned words of Kochi Reza and others of her generation, or the younger poets who are finding their voice, we are left with a feeling of wanting more. Rather than nationalism as a constraining, jingoistic notion, these poems are a celebration of Bangladesh from a women's gaze, giving due recognition to the injustice, colonisation, upheavals and neglect that those who have been part of this land have faced, along with that which has given them a resilience, and a certain kind of defiance and multiplicity.

Most importantly, the women in this collection come across as the multi-dimensional beings we are; beyond binary caricatures. Historically, 'ma', the mother, has been put on a 'pedestal', given the 'highest' position; the one who gives and sacrifices, is devoted to her family, but rarely is expected to have dreams or thoughts of her own. The counter of this is the lack of rights and social acceptance for women actually demanding their voices be heard and their rights to be respected, and their potential to be met. Throughout the ages we have demonized or glorified women with a 'bad' woman/'good' woman narrative. Women have been used as cultural markers to represent the horrors of the war with a 'loss of honour' as women who were raped, or vilified for the violation of their bodies being their fault.

From strident voices of strong women who pioneered the way, encapsulating the fervour of rebellion, whether it is from those who were born well before the war of independence, like Sufia Kamal and Anwara Syed Haq, to those who had their formative years in Bangladesh like Leesa Gazi, and Shahnaz Munni, to the newer voices of Rimjhim Ahmed, Mahi Flora and Shweta Shatabdi Esh, the collection traverses generations, with surprises and twists along the way.

The modernity of the work spans the collection. From the trepidations of love, seen through Farida Majid's *The Wait*, or Taslima Nasrin's *Emancipation*, to Zeenat Ara Rafiq's powerful *Promise*, and Anjana Saha's *The Curse*, with Alaka Nandita's refreshing *Eye Glasses*, and Shakira Parvin's stark *Special*, as well as Shanta Maria's irreverently 'spot on' *What's a Woman Gotta Do in Heaven*, to the quirky, off left field *Crime* from Jahanara Perveen, and *Existentialism* of Novera Hossain, these gems, largely unknown to the wider world, along with the many more poems in this collection, underline the contrast between truth and perception, countering stereotypes and defying societal restrictions.

The poems capture women as I have known many to be in all my years here—passionate in love and purpose, compassionate, courageous, unconventional, not taking no for an answer, full of rage against the unfair structures that be, and wanting to tackle the world at large on their own terms, along with expressing vulnerabilities and acknowledging the tribulations of fighting deep-rooted patriarchy and prejudice. There is a feeling that perhaps the elegance and cadence of their words can only be fully appreciated in the original Bangla. However, this translated collection does convey the philosophical and the practical, and I believe will entice and inspire lovers of poetry to dig deeper and further explore their works, and those of other Bangladeshi women poets (those who write in Bangla, English and the myriad of other local languages) too.

Sadaf Saaz
Poet, Director & Producer
Dhaka Lit Fest

Dhaka
December 2021

Curator's Introduction

Bangladesh won her independence in 1971 through a bloody war of liberation and is celebrating the golden jubilee of her glorious emergence this year. During that deadly and devastating war of independence, the women of Bangladesh in particular paid a hefty toll. Even though they fought side by side with their male counterparts, they were the first victims of the invading Pakistani army and their local cohorts. They were killed, tortured, mutilated, and worst of all, raped en masse by the marauding army. As many as two-hundred-thousand women fell prey to unprecedented and unbridled brutality. After independence, these women were given an honorific title, *Birangona*, or War Heroine, by the father of the nation, Bangabandhu Sheikh Mujibur Rahman, in recognition of their suffering and sacrifice.

During the year-long celebration of her golden jubilee, Bangladesh saw a plethora of events and activities to commemorate the historic landmark. Unfortunately, nothing very significant was planned at the national level to pay tribute to the heroic women who fought and suffered, were persecuted and murdered, and who contributed immensely to the struggle for freedom and independence. As a writer, translator, and literary activist I was curious to see if the Bangladeshi publishing sector was doing anything worthwhile focusing on women, and from their own perspective, to celebrate this hugely important event. Sadly, this too proved to be extremely male-centric with hundreds of publications focused mainly on history, politics, memoirs, poetry, fiction, etc., written mostly by male authors, and predictably purely from a male point of view. This disheartened me deeply.

At that point, knowing my interest in women's literature, both global and local, my Kolkata-based friend, Venkateswar Ramaswamy, a Tamil-speaker who is a literary translator from Bengali, who harbours an intense love for the Bengali language, and Bangladeshi literature in particular, urged me to compile an anthology of 50 women poets of Bangladesh, translated into English, in commemoration of the 50th anniversary of Bangladesh. This idea immediately caught my attention, but at the beginning I was a little apprehensive about committing myself to this rather grand proposition, considering the enormity of this daunting task. But after some persuasion on Ramaswamy's part, and some intense soul-searching of my own, I relented. And thus began this beautiful trans-border literary project, which gained its own momentum when Nabina Das, a critically acclaimed English-language poet from India and a fine translator in her own right, agreed to come on board, enthusiastically undertaking the mammoth task of translating the selected poems into English. It needs to be reiterated here that India as a neighbouring country played a pivotal role in 1971, and was instrumental in the emergence of Bangladesh as an independent nation.

The first and formidable challenge was of course to select the 50 poets to be anthologised. Deciding on the timeframe was relatively easier since the occasion was to celebrate the 50 years of the creation of an independent Bangladesh. Hence the obvious criterion was that we would begin with the senior-most woman poet who was still alive and actively writing in independent Bangladesh. And then we would continue chronologically till the most recent period and choose one of the youngest woman poets as our closing entry, someone who has earned some reputation and readership in the country. The first entry for me was obvious: Begum Sufia Kamal (1911-1999). She was not only the most widely known and admired veteran woman poet of our newly independent nation, but also had been at the forefront of the struggle for independence, beginning from the historic Bengali language movement back in the 1950s. She was also very vocal for women's rights and empowerment, and considered to be the foremost spokesperson of the women's liberation movement in pre- and post-independence Bangladesh.

From the initial list of around hundred poets of varying age, temperament, poetic sensibility, writing style and of course, the content of their poetry, I had to sift through very carefully, treading a delicate path, to make the final selection of the 50 poets being presented here. The bottom line was to make the anthology representative of independent Bangladesh and her established literary ethos as much as possible, without compromising on the quality of the poems and the historical contribution of the poets in defining the contemporary poetry scene of Bangladesh. And thus, we came to pick our last entry, Shweta Shatabdi Esh, who in her late twenties, and fighting a severe physical ailment, has published quite a few noteworthy collections and earned a prestigious literary award as well.

And in between we had the privilege to include a few freedom-fighter poets too. The most noteworthy among them is of course Meherun Nesa (1942-1971), a working-class poet who was actively involved with the pro-independence, progressive political movement, and had to pay the price for it with her life. She was brutally slaughtered by the invaders during the ruthless military crackdown in Dhaka in the days of March 1971. Kazi Rozi, another valiant warrior poet, crossed the border during the liberation war and joined the clandestine radio known as *Swadhin Bangla Betar Kendra*, or Free Bengal Radio Station, to continue her campaign for liberty through the power of poetry, both written and spoken. Suraiya Khanum (1944-2006), an early modernist of post-war Bangladeshi poetry, was also a vocal supporter of the liberation war who campaigned against the Pakistani brutality vehemently in London, UK, throughout 1971, while a graduate student there. The same is true about Farida Majid

(1942-2021), a translator, editor, and a first-generation Bangladeshi poet, who wrote in English. She was a force to reckon with during the 1971 pro-Bangladesh movement in London, for her exceptional organizing capacity as well as many other contributions. It is a pity that she did not live to see the publication of this anthology as she lost her long battle with cancer only a few months back. We pause for a moment here to remember and recognize her immense contribution towards Bengali language and literature, and pay our best tributes to the departed soul.

Among other stalwarts featured in this anthology, Anwara Syed Haq, a psychologist and prolific author of both prose and poetry, is the senior-most living woman writer in present-day Bangladesh, and is widely known for her radical feminist views. Another fiercely feminist writer represented here, the internationally known author Taslima Nasrin, now living in forced exile for almost 30 years, also deserves special mention. We deem it a necessary obligation to raise our voice here in appeal to the appropriate authority, to allow her to return to Bangladesh and end her long and traumatic exile to pursue her literary career in a more familiar and favourable milieu. We are also happy to feature Nasima Sultana (1957-1997), a brave new voice of contemporary Bangladeshi poetry who was bent upon breaking away from the age-old shackles of tradition and taboos imposed on women by the male chauvinist, patriarchal society. Unfortunately, her life was also cut short by cancer. We hope that this anthology will act as a catalyst in renewing interest in her extraordinary life and work, particularly among the younger generation who hardly know about this truly talented poet of the country.

The toughest part of the project, however, was to select the actual poems to be translated. This whole process took place during the height of the pandemic, in a complete locked-down situation—interestingly, we also have a poem titled "Locked Down" in this anthology—which made it extremely difficult to collect the books of the selected poets. Thanks to some of the poets themselves, who were kind enough to send me an assortment of their poems over email, I could make an initial headway. For some other entries, I'm grateful to the rich literary magazine, *Mananrekha*, which brought out a special volume on the women poets of Bangladesh a few years back. This came in very handy in finding the poems of some of the poets who were no longer alive, and whose books and/or poems are not readily available now. I take this opportunity to thank its editor, Professor Mizanur Rahman Nasim, who very kindly sent me a copy of the magazine from faraway Rangpur, the northernmost district of Bangladesh. Finally, for the poems of the poets of the younger generation, most of whom weren't personally known to me, I had to depend heavily on another young poet, Sabera Tabassum, who along with two of her poet friends runs *Poetry Platform*, an exceptional organization of women poets. She recommended some of the poets included in this collection, contacted them personally on my behalf, obtained their consent and, of course, the poems themselves. This really made my task easier and allowed me to complete the selection process quickly and without much trouble, something I was very apprehensive about. I express my heartfelt thanks and gratitude to Sabera Tabassum, for without her unconditional support it wouldn't have been possible for me to put these poems together in the form of a truly representative anthology.

But I must hasten to admit that owing to all the constraints imposed by the deadly pandemic, the poems selected here are by no means the very best of the work of the respective authors. However, we can vouch that they are certainly of a high literary quality and can definitely be categorized as somewhat representative of the poets' oeuvres. While we take pride in being a pioneer of sorts in compiling this one-of-a-kind anthology of Bangladeshi women poets at a very auspicious moment of our history, we are also well aware of some of its obvious lacunae and limitations, which we would like to address and overcome through future editions. For now, we leave it to the readers and critics to judge our accomplishments and failings alike, with a sincere hope that this modest anthology will act as a reliable reference point and as a springboard for more such undertakings in future, larger in scope and more comprehensive in nature.

In conclusion, I would like to thank many of the poets and editors represented here for their kind cooperation; Nabina Das, the translator of the poems presented here, for her painstaking work, not just in translating the poems so meticulously but also for continuous communication and coordination with many publishers and literary editors; Cecily Chen and Roh-Suan Tung of Balestier Press, for lending their full support to this project; Sadaf Saaz, acclaimed poet writing in English, and founder-director of the prestigious Dhaka Lit Fest, for agreeing to write the foreword; Deborah Smith and Vivek Narayanan for their cover blurbs; art scholars Rezaul Karim Sumon and Shikoa Nazneen, for their valuable advice and help with the cover design, Gregoire de Brouhns, husband of late Novera Ahmed, for giving us the permission on behalf of Museum Novera Ahmed, Paris, to use the image of one of her artworks in the cover, and also some others such as expatriate writer Abedin Quader, my photographer friend Johora Bebe Ira, poet and translator Razu Alauddin, poet and editor Ali Afzal Khan, poet Megh Aditi, fiction writer Shumi Sikander, et al, for their help in connecting with some of the poets to collect their poems for the anthology.

I rest my case with a very timely and befitting victory chant: Long live Bangladesh! Long live literature! Long live poetry!

Alam Khorshed
Chittagong, Bangladesh
December 2021

Translator's Note

Translation of poetry is always a strange landscape one traverses. Legs and hands are needed to crawl, scratch, run, or even punch. At times one might need to do a cartwheel. Perhaps a hop skip and jump. Head butting is allowed too, as is kicking, and occasionally one swims across in whatever manner one can. The stage of survival. At the end of it, many methods exhausted, just lie down and breathe, become a 'shav'—a dead body—not dead per se, but detached and quiet as one. Breathe.

What I'm talking about here is the sheer physical labour involved in translations. There is the other stage once we start breathing. The stage of discovery/recovery.

To smell the topography of the language of poetry, to hear flutters and rumbles of verbs, to lick the sudden honey or dew or even salty tear drops of emotions, or to see how meanings and metaphors change shapes and colours in a cognitive carnival, it goes a long way to discover what comes when the translated text that survived assumes a life of its own.

In the context of this anthology of 50 Bangladeshi women poets to commemorate the glorious 50th anniversary of Bangladesh, the sights, smells, sounds, etc., are connected to more than just one life form. It's a whole universe, many lives that crystallised to form a veritable feast, a throbbing sentient body of poetry, imbued with hope and as one poet said, still 'growing defiant'. But to meet that body, it took me time to locate the archaeology of my own roots, the materials of my own poetic landscape.

It was early 2021 in Kolkata one morning—the terrible covid-19 lockdown had somewhat been relaxed for travels and essential work then—friend and literary translator V Ramaswamy and I were discussing poetry and the perils of doing an anthology. At that time, I was deeply immersed in and itching to finish a humongous anthology of 'dissent poetry' showcasing 250 poets from the length and breadth of India. When Ramaswamy—an ardent translator of several Bengali fiction, the most significant till date being the Subimal Mishra novels—suggested translating 50 women poets from Bangladesh in the light of the ongoing golden jubilee celebrations of Bangladesh as a nation, my first reaction was—yes, great, but not me. I was positive that after my current back-breaking assignment, I cannot take up even five poets for any new project, let alone 50. Looking back, I think I didn't commit to the proposal, but I didn't firmly say a 'no' either.

Apart from the exhaustion from my ongoing editing, the lengthy pandemic, and other issues of life and livelihood, I was quite sure, translating 50 Bangladeshi women poets within a short span—since the proposal came to me when the 50th celebrations of Bangladesh were already underway—and to publish a book to mark the historic event on time was next to impossible. I had translated poetry earlier from the Assamese and Bengali, but not for an entire book, and not at this pace. Nothing short of another whole year to achieve this, I mulled.

Also the idea of nation or nationhood was not quite my cup of tea, be it India or Bangladesh or any other country. The idea of borders was an anathema to me, and I saw nation states as an exercise justifying wars and further oppression, as modern history might tell us in copious examples. Tagore's epithet of nationalism being "carnivorous and cannibalistic" rings true when we look around and see how nations treat their very own people miserably and unjustly, women being the first casualty. The subcontinent is a testimony to innumerable such ills, including conflicts, hostilities, and wars among its various 'national' borders. Any nationalistic cause, therefore, was not conducive to creating literary zeal in me.

But during this time, I spoke to my mother Krishna Das who is currently the sole purveyor of stories from e-paar (this side) and o-paar (that side) Bengal, and she enthusiastically spoke of what she knew of the land she left behind, as it became Bangladesh, not just a nation but a realization of dreams held by millions against atrocities and occupation. Through social media I was also reading occasional notes from my older cousin Dr Dibalok Singha, a Bangladeshi citizen, recalling the sacrifices and struggles around that period his mother Anima Singh—my paternal aunt—and his father Moni Singh, former chairperson, Communist Party of Bangladesh, had undertaken along with several cadres, freedom fighters, and indigenous leaders. Stories I knew, and stories that I was learning more about, in newer lights.

It is through Ramaswamy that I made acquaintance with acclaimed writer, translator, and art critic Alam Khorshed, of Bistaar: Chittagong Arts Complex. He is the avid curator of the poems in this book, an impressive range of work. By then, my interest had grown in the work of Bangladeshi women poets. And we all came on board.

While the poems started to accumulate in my mail box, the real translation was yet to begin. I did not possess a complete Bengali or a Bengali-English dictionary. My own Bengali was also another frontier where I was a little conflicted. Born and brought up in Guwahati, Assam, I wasn't native to Bengal or its culture and language. I was a bilingual, who spoke, wrote, and read both Assamese and Bengali. My earlier translations of poetry included Assamese poetry, but not book-length, and a few Bengali poems of my own. I was mostly comfortable now writing in English. The 50 Bangladeshi poets would be challenging, given there were poets ranging from the 1930s to the present day, embodying a vast range of emotions and ideas, as well as diction. The responsibility was massive.

As the translator of this book, I saw my contribution as an enabler of cross-border literary alliances and neighbourly goodwill. In the era of globalization, while a lot remains to be done for our respective nations, it goes without saying that a convergence of ideas across the borders is a solid way of foregrounding our common concerns. Literature for me, as a poet and author, is a sure roadmap for forging ties that poetry alone perhaps can achieve. Here I had to be aware of the fact that in the post-colonial literary plane of the subcontinent, Bangladesh was on a unique trajectory she set for herself. Her history was refracted like sunlight through water—she had gained freedom that was non-linear, and hence, complex and richer than her neighbours.

Once I was briefly asked—what is my methodology in translating literary work? I had replied briefly that I needed to ingest the source text until it flew in my veins. Such grand metaphor apart, I really felt the original poems could reappear as translations only after I had chewed them well. July-August 2021 was a most bizarre phase in my life when I realized that since more than a year, I had not written any poetry barring one short series after the Covid-19 lockdown of 2020. I was agonised, and pining to get back to poetry, to anyone or anything that might save my life by letting poetry come back to me.

I fished out the scanned poems from my inbox and began reading them, at odd hours. I read back and forth, without any particular method, skipping chronology. At times I read a poem more than thrice, and often aloud. Borges' famous utterance that the "original is unfaithful to the translation" played in my head, and I kept wooing the poems one by one (an unfaithful translator at last, a traitor as some other translation theorist might say)!

The 50 Bangladeshi women poets in this anthology represent a diverse style. The older poets among this group are especially reminiscent of Bangla poetics that is common to both the Bengals—e-paar (this side) and o-paar (that side) mentioned earlier—in terms of geographical and cultural ethos. The poets that come up later, from lyrical to highly realistic ones, represent a Bangladesh in the throes of political, economic, and social upheavals. In the midst of all this there is also the phoenix-like surge in idioms and images in the work of the poets from the periods that saw military rule, sectarian violence, and scuttling of democracy in Bangladesh. Among the younger poets, the poetry blooms in many directions, when the women poets are more aware of their condition, their rights, and of emancipation as part of a radical change in the polity of the country. The latter's language offers a striking blend of modernity and humanistic ethos. To name the poets selectively would be a lapse on my part, but since the book is chronologically arranged, Sufia Kamal's voice stands out as strident and radical as we begin to read, a beacon in Bangladeshi poetry. The youngest and the final poet in our list Shweta Shatabdi Esh challenges with her overlapping images and crisp style. Meherun Nesa stands out singularly as the working class poet who reaffirms our faith in beauty and resurrection amid terrible violence unleashed by anti-liberation forces (to which she fell), her work a testimony to the dreams of the toiling masses.

I complained here earlier about not possessing a dictionary and it took only a while to remember again what Borges had said–"The dictionary is based on the hypothesis—obviously an unproven one —that languages are made up of equivalent synonyms." There was no doubt such a hypothesis would only jeopardise my reading of the women poets of Bangladesh. And traitor that I was, junking theories of nation and opting for cross-border alliances, language for me here was made up of historical sensibilities of defiance, cultural and semiotic convergences, and poetic praxis. I was chewing manna.

When I finally began translating the poems in September 2021, I'd already ingested them to a great extent. And because I remembered Umberto Eco saying somewhere that "translation is the art of failure", I became fearless. Poets and poetry and failure? Clearly, there is more to translations than just (even brilliant) men preaching about it! Translation for me is the art of conversation, when poetry and the poet as a translator find that spatial-temporal niche to exchange ideas and notes. Conversations don't fail, they continue.

Even then Walter Benjamin came close to what I felt while translating these poems, 'to liberate the language imprisoned in a work' in my 'recreation of that work', the only difference being I didn't perceive the target language to be imprisoned in the source work. In the end, my bilingual disposition—peppered by English and other language fluency—helped.

The technical aspects of translating poetry are akin to practicing music—each end rhyme, each note, each cadence to be tested and voiced over and over again. For instance, the title poem of this volume 'Benibinyash shomoy to aar nei' ('Arise Out of the Lock') teased me with possibilities. The poet's tone of exhortation was so strong that the image of a woman and her coiffure, deftly woven with the central theme of rebellion, immediately led me to imagine how 'lock' have multiple performatives here. Renouncing caring for her lock of hair —making a beni or a plait—as an idle pursuit, and breaking the lock of oppression—Sufia Kamal's poem gave me this rich metaphor of the woman gearing up for the war of liberation as well as to fight the patriarchy, an overwhelming reality in the history of Bangladesh. This poem is in rhymed couplets, as is 'Enigma' (Prahelika) by Shelly Naz. My attempt to keep the end rhymes turned out to be an exercise in introspection—how slant, half or full rhymes can be extracted out in translation, keeping the meaning intact. It's about textuality, how the essence of text transmits itself to the translator and then to the reader.

The only set of haiku in this volume by Rahima Akhter Kalpana is poignant in its resonance of the ambiance of Bengal and Bengali. Showcasing the nuance of the ten pieces required a studied understanding of the poet's mood of "zen"—spirituality—and "hosomi"—delicate sensitivity. From a Japanese form to Bengali haiku trans-created into English, these are fine etchings and measured utterances.

I've left several Bengali words as it is, whereas some I have translated. In this I trusted my instinct. Where birds, flowers, trees, items of cultural significance, and names exuded mystery and music, I let it stay. I rendered the rest into English because the poems' schema or the essence demanded it. Regarding punctuations, I followed the poet's lead, and added mine only where the rhetorical need arose, following English syntax rules.

Traversing this vast topography of 100-odd poems, while physically I laboured and translated nearly eighty per cent of the poems by the first fortnight of September itself, the sight-smell-touch-hear journey had just begun. Other than the iconic Bengal landscape of fleecy kaash flowers, rippling wide rivers, autumn's mellow skies, and the aroma of Hilsa and rice, the heady fragrance of jasmine and hasnahana, and more, the ethno-cultural heritage of the poets in this book defy all borders, state-sanctioned injunctions, and stereotypes. From allusions—whether Islamic or Hindu or Buddhist—to epics, festivals, myths, and magic, the women poets here speak in a syncretic voice. These are the women that I have known from family lore and books —as freedom-loving, courageous, lovelorn, compassionate, just, and fierce individuals (my aunt "krishak netri or peasant leader" Anima Singh being one). I was reading history told the way it should be, in women's voices.

We could do more I suppose, search out the LGBTQ voices (so hard to locate in a milieu where they're considered a taboo), and also include poets from Bangladesh's indigenous communities for that unique perspective. We would need to do another critical book.

Whenever I needed help understanding bits and pieces in this challenging body of work, Alam Khorshed, the tireless curator, was always available. My mother gave her cultural inputs when specific contexts arose while translating. Deborah Smith of Tilted Axis Press (UK) whose contact came via the brilliant poet Rohan Chhetri, readily gave us a shout-out. Poet and translator Vivek Narayanan offered solid words of appreciation. Sadaf Saaz, poet and founder-director of the world-renowned Dhaka Lit Fest, wrote for us a brilliant foreword summing up all what I felt within myself in this journey of translations.

Finally, I'm delighted that Cecily Chen and Roh-Sung Tung of Balestier Press (UK) offered us a contract within days of our querying, and all along sent unbridled praise for the work. I'd also like to thank friend Kala Ramesh, an acclaimed haiku master, and director of Triveni Haikai India, for her insights in my quest for translating haiku from Bengali to English. Last but not the least, the 50 Bangladeshi women poets helped me liberate my language, and any time I stumbled over words or expressions, wooing the poems over again assured a pleasurable breakthrough, a parley of love.

The job of writing or translating is a solitary one, a struggle for sure. The haloed architect and visionary of Bangladesh, Bangabandhu Sheikh Mujibur Rahman had said in his historic March 7, 1971, speech: "This time the struggle is for our freedom, this time the struggle is for our independence! Joy Bangla!"

Fifty years down the line, I interpret this utterance in a wider cultural and literary context. Translation is struggle, and through it, freedom comes in greater scopes—that which encompasses unheard voices, resistance, and women's and people's dreams and aspirations. As the translator, my goal and personal gain is to be a part of that struggle.

Nabina Das
Hyderabad, India
January 2022

Arise out of the Lock

SUFIA KAMAL (1911-1999)

Arise out of the Lock

No time to braid that lock, to arise is the order!
Whether or not the sari has a graceful border,
the beauty mark on the forehead, kajal[1] in eyes, time
to redden your lips is up, it's over. It's life or death rings the chime.
No more just smiling teenagers, young women, and wives:
defined chin, mouth and lips firm, to pledge and strive,
forever alert. Just as the bright sharp sabre
wide eyes raised quick to the moment, not lowered any more.
No longer frightened like the doe, those glances, hark,
show a mind in search, a falcon looking for its mark.
Their hearts sans mercy, hardened like solid stone
to wield revenge against the invaders of our home.
The woman's shy soft form has gone for a change,
all her dear ones, kin, and comrades she will now avenge.
Slim waist and her bosom full of the lion's might
the brave-heart holds boundless strength, no love songs in voice bright.
Hail Motherland, hail the people! Glory be to the Muktisena[2], hail!
Her aanchal[3] soaked in martyrs' blood, the woman too is ready to sail.

Unseasonal Cloud

Overcast with clouds here—
the Dhaka sky is full of clouds—
this cloud has come from across the southern sea,
where your sighs
accumulated day to day and greying
                      they've spread over the sky,
now have come like clouds, like compassion,
like the thoughts in your mind.
That is why it keeps melting down in my long sighs—
from the touch of pain flowing from your mind.
As though it has come gliding along the path of the sky within me,
as a cloud-beauty, overwhelming my eyes!
Melting clouds, clouds as droplets,
                each speck of the cloud
like your touch has wrought gold
                  all over my body.
As brilliant as diamond shavings
it has all showered on my cheeks
                  mingled with my tears.
This hour is the hour of pain, when in the sky
                  clouds build up
in the Dhaka sky, in your sky, in my sky.
Do our minds fill with a charming lull?
This morning, in this unseasonal time
clouds build up in the Dhaka sky.

KHALEDA EDIB CHOWDHURY (1937-2008)

Palmful of Dreams

The lengthening shadows stand here, shy, hesitating
because the tree is meek, the leaves all fall in mourning
the benumbed dry wind throbs, water gurgles—
they murmur quietly—I'm there in palmful of dreams.

The last road-marks are washed out—seeds die in germination
the beak with a bird-call rustles amid leaves
a poison quarry hides in the cavern of the heart,
stay in silence, you faraway jasmine-star.

All compassion spent, the long night wanes
love is so pale, sheathed away who even knew.
Birds don't know where to go, this dust-blown world
the flame of pain upholds the lustre of the rising sun.

Today I stand on the vast sandy land
in darkness with empty hands, in an imperilled wonder,
it'll go to oblivion, or be a remembrance for some
in the murmur of the forest will love lie unseen.

A Life Passes

This one life of mine passes
from light, from dreams
someone asks me to bow low
after my journey is completed in the last hour of the noon.

The way a life passes
the way a life waves to you
just for the need of this life of mine in genuflection—

I do not know what is that blind arrangement
I do not know in the lake of life immersion of lotuses and lilies
I do not know mourning and regret
within me a song of fallen leaves of the waning times—

I suppose this is how it passes
to bow low like this, this slipping hour of mine
in the known and unknown of planets of beyond a timid lethargy in dreams.

Where will I find another life?
Where do people find one?
Alas, as the swamps drown the dilemma of sorrows,
the kiss of grass in the last mist of autumn
where shall I find life.
After a life passes
beyond the boundaries of another life I'll be gone
unbeknownst to dreams and bereavement.

ANWARA SYED HAQ (*b.* 1940)

To a Woman Called Heart

This me that you see
everything on her is on loan.
The bright intricate design and the stitch of her attire
the aanchal with fine-woven flowers, zari[4] work on the borders
the eye-catching blossoms motif of the blouse
the one to claim all this beauty is the worker of Mirpur.
This me that you look at wearing spiffy sunshades
emitting rays, hairclip of peacock hues,
fancy curvy footwear, all these items are borrowed.
Basically, none of the objects on my body are mine
these eyes are on loan, this head is another's skull
this liver, the pair of kidneys, intestines or bowels
they're functioning solely at the mercy of the others;
these lungs are breathing, but this is borrowed
breath from someone else.
Nothing at all in this body is mine
even the skin has been grafted from foreign money grants.

There's only one entity I have kept aside carefully
in extreme secrecy, with a lot of clever cover up
in rain's water-stairs, in the eternal flow of consciousness
in fast moving cars away from people's eyes
concealed from Ravan's aggressive eyes
in utmost wisdom tucked inside the deep cavity of my bosom:
a woman called heart.

Life is Not Entirely a Clean Slate

Life is not entirely a clean slate
some stains have remained here and there
some regrets took shelter in the lower drawer of the table
some days and nights were spent in debauchery
some deception, lies, some indecent acts, greasing of the palms
left relentless scratches and lines on the floor carpet.
Life didn't turn out to be a clean slate.

Although early morning I wished to gather only white shiuli blossoms
a few worms, muck, slimy maggots
got tossed in with the shiuli's[5] whiteness
in effect time elapsed in between things dark and soiled
some more gone in hesitation, dilemma, and fear;
life wasn't entirely a clean slate.

Some moss and water hyacinth covered the pondside steps
some bickering, competition, jealousy, and mocking
more unsaid things overcame the mind
now at the hour of departure 'life isn't entirely a clean slate'
is the lament I keep hearing here and there.

This life is after all human life
white and dark plaited along the tresses
our human lives.

FARIDA MAJID (1942-2021)

In This Way

I wouldn't have been destroyed this way
if inside the darkened fist of
yellow curled mallika petals I could sleep.
I wouldn't ever have been decimated
if on the broken marble stone of the Parthenon
under the dense shade of pine trees, in step with big black ants
I could walk in a straight line.

In my empty mind, thoughtless
when I doze
at times my index finger quietly curls up
to touch softly the tip of my thumb.
At the moment of that touch in sheer ecstasy I turn into infinity.
The ants on the stairs of the Parthenon then mean nothing to me.
On the hot sand of the pyramid the giant
blue beetle I saw lying
even that is nothing.

What fears this earth has, and everything is dark.
Only if relaxed within the shaded fist
of curled up yellow mallika[6] petals
I could fall asleep, then
I wouldn't be destroyed in this manner.

The Wait

Why did you become a friend?
Why did you not beckon me on the beach at sunset hour?
At the call of sea gulls returning to their nest,
before we slumped into a deep intoxicating slumber?

Again I'm sitting alone with a glass in hand,
on the bar stool where everyone's leaving.
I haven't dozed off yet. Hello? Call me!

In the delicatessen too across the road
business has crashed. They'll close the books
bring down the iron gate, place a padlock.
Then they'll leave extinguishing from
the sight another superfluous light.
Yelping like a street dog being kicked around
the garbage truck has stopped at the crossing
at the red light's blink.

The barman has washed all the dirty glasses.
The one I'm holding is yet to be done
still there are a few minutes left.
Hello? Call me!

MEHERUN NESA (1942-1971)

To the Flower and the Moon

1.
I don't have a garden, I hanker for flowers
the sapling in the pot only flowers in ones or twos—
that barely quenches the core of my desire.
Then do not bloom this way, flowers,
do not make my flower-soul restless
tell me how do I fulfil this garden-desire
of mine planting only saplings in pots?

2.
Whatever others say, you be my moon
atop the bamboo grove, in any such manner
when I sorely miss Kajla Didi[7], grieve her.
How do I say how much I need you?
Not a burnt roti to me, you are not,
even if the earth is harsher than ever–
in speckless metaphors may you thrive
like the half-veiled face in the chamber, Bengal's bride.

A Portrait of Darkness

A desolate night steeped in deep fog
the electric light bulb conjures ghostly shadows,
deserted roads, somewhere sudden bark of hungry dogs,
in the stunned darkness of a dead nature
an unspoken rush.

In this unresponsive domain of time
awake through the night all alone
through the throat and ribcage
whose hands creep out like tongs?
They rapidly come up to snuff
off the life of coming days,
to kill life that draws portraits
on a shadow-less canvas of the earth.

Still I forcefully remove that grasp
by the brave hand of my mind
I wake up to see a new sunshine
on a fresh new morn.
Nights wane, days dawn
the cycle of season turns twelve months
the one that doesn't turn, at winter's end
like the days of early spring
are those oncoming days of life
stricken by sorrow and pain.

The desolate night steeped in deep fog
a mechanical pace on the dial of my watch
I toy with this sleepless time
with tact and play.

ZEENAT ARA RAFIQ (1944-2005)

Promise

Destruction is beautiful
destruction is very beautiful
fearfully phenomenal.
This quiet afternoon
    lifeless

History will not put its signature on such days.
These idle clouds
mango trees wrapped in fragrant flowering buds
and the buzz of inert bees:
instead let storms come striking down the earth's bosom,
let it plunder the tree branches
    let vultures descend shrieking

And gathered from that apocalyptic moment
    the terrible promise in your eyes:
    and on your sad countenance
the mad dance of soft dry reddish mop of hair.

Evening Ode

Dead fish with feculent eyes
cold coloured water
and a few hawks in the sky—
evening ode is all about them.

Not the beauty emanating from wisdom
not the light radiating from unknown flower bouquets
                    not about them.
These others, those that do not demand anything, let
me compose odes about them.

Walking Along

This path of mine I alone have to traverse
far—far, very far, the flowers of shaal[8] and shimul[9], in bunches
in the blooming forests of krishnachuda[10] and jarul[11].
Together with it the cement-paved walking trail

the cold dead poetry of dust from a light cover in flight
I will have to fly close to the peak of the silvery moon,
traversing hostile hard paths of hills, freezing water of rivers.

SURAIYA KHANUM (1944-2006)

Nursing Home

Look here, body of mine.
This is like your abode of peace and purification,
this is like a rest house, O passer-by, tired way-farer
do be seated on the spread out sheetal-paati[12]
amid rose water sprinkles, under the jackfruit shade!

Look here, heart of mine:
your shawl of sorrow
soiled clothes and all else worn
peel off and hang them on this warm clothes-hanger
loosen the buttons of the past:
I'm the mirror, look here and see
keep yourself in my shadow, way-farer!

Sit here, mind:
I'm my own comb, mind
I'll untangle your dreadlocks of sorrow right now!

Warm yourself in my oven
all of what you have, and heal!

Interrogation

Seven blind dwarfs, they groped me all over
all seven of them check me out in seven ways
angered, they pierced my chest with seven poison needles
kicked me seven times
and they kissed me seven kisses,
these seven blind dwarfs.
Like blinds they asked me:
Hey tell, tell who you are, who are you?

I was lying down then with my head in the sky
seven stars kept playing in my hair.

Solitary Travel

Each time I've gone to dip my toes in the cursed Yamuna
fierce shark teeth have bruised me, and
I was swept away all alone in the peaking waves of Gorky[13]!

By the time I'm back in the hustle of settlements, it gets dark
the bridge of time collapses!
So many innocent ayat[14] verses have gone asunder;
so many scratches, rude strikes on my golden mirror!

Every time I carry my pitcher and return to hearths,
hark, snake, cry panic-stricken people in flight!

Within the crystal white sparkle of this mind and body
do they see any hint of ruin, envy, or destruction?

RUBI RAHMAN (*b.* 1946)

Watch If You Can

Let her be, just see, what all she can do
no home or hearth, no sense whatsoever; don't marry her.
She can hardly run a household!
Just try once, set a test for her—see if she's capable or not
give her a lapsed bank cheque then watch what happens
she definitely will buy you
square kerchief-shaped yellow mustard fields, dancing rivers…
Please do believe she is quite dutiful—
the other morning I saw her heading to the vegetable market
carrying a cart full of fallen dry leaves.
She'll mix the green of lettuce in the red of tomatoes
and present a Qayyum[15] easel to the lady of the house
this you know, you completely will agree.
A few garden full of butterflies in your apartment rooms
a field full of shining fireflies if you want she'll bring in a jiffy.

For her do bring from the eternal infinite Mahakaal[16]
a couple of mornings.
Next to her dinner plate leave a little slice of moon in a blue bowl
even next to penury get for her all the cuckoos of springtime;
do not ask why give, if you can, but give her these liberties.
Do keep her outside the calculations of a quick marriage
she'll scrounge through Glasnost[17] and perhaps fetch you a true human world;
give her an elaborate wedding, some concessions
and make for her a path paved towards beauty.

Life

I sit down with pen and paper to write down the truths of life
I want to give up everything and go far away, move away
I swim across past-present like a slim fish
I grind myself against the stone as though I'm of sandalwood.

At my table burning midnight oil
I compose life from pounding my bones and marrow;
my little girl leaves for school caressed by the morning light
I hold her hand and see next to my table
life sprinting fast, quick-footed.

KAZI ROZI (*b.* 1949)

I Can't

I have numerous ways of saying I can't
for example—I can't be happy speaking another tongue, another flavour
like barns filled with rice grains, ponds full of fish
Bangla alphabets would be the ones to fill all darkness.

In the heart of a boxed up darkness
Bangla alphabets emitting light and brightness;
unless shining from them I don't find comfort in lights.
The earth trembles at the great sound impact
like the sky-ripping thunder of the clouds,
the terra firma shakes, the ocean too.
The chorus that ensues from
what my vowels and consonants play in the heart's quiet harbour
that sound alone keeps me happy.

I have numerous ways of saying I can't.
But won't explain it all now, today I just want to say—
I simply cannot live without my Bangla, I won't.

Ornament

In a still-water pond
a woman had searched for her face
most of her face was obscured by ornaments.

The sky took off her ornaments
clouds showered down
the moon unhooked her ornaments
the moonlight melted off
even the woman shed all her ornaments
she became only a woman.

The woman gave the sky ornaments made of stars
to the moon she gave ornaments made of the night
man gave the woman ornaments of wars
ornaments of blood bequeathed to life.

Now woman means
the male sun of an unadorned sky,
man means the woman's tidy courtyard;
after all ornaments of wars are shed,
now a man's ornament is the sun
a woman's ornament is the creative woman herself.

ZARINA AKHTER (b. 1951)

No

Like a solid strong pillar the word "no"
stands firmly before all my destinations—
but it doesn't mean that
I will never fight
I will never fall in love
will not listen to songs.

But of course
if you say—the way this civilisation is stomping ahead clearing forests
give it legitimacy
I will say—'No'.
If you say—the market is stocked with commodities
why don't you buy a pretty peacock feather and come fancy-dressed
I will say—'No'.
If you say—there in that closed-door room ignorant traders are holding a meeting
just bend down your head once and whatever petition you have
present it there—everything will be granted
I will say—'No'.

Poet and the Cook

About to temper the hot wok with paanch foron[18] on the stove
suddenly my hand halts—
like the lover-god Kanai[19], poetry sneaks up at my shoulder
whispering in my ears he reminds me of the half-done poem
and that's it
oil water spices vegetables—everything gets muddled
my mind begins to race across faraway fields
in search of golden grains tucked in words,
bewitched by kaash's[20] eternal beauty this heart forgets all cooking,
certainly there is no fear of anyone's scorn
but there's fear of chagrin from the man of the house;
the poem is waiting just for one right word
unable to reach its home—
the shame of this failure filling my senses makes me crazy,
say, what would you have done?
You would've caught that word by its neck
from rocking away idly on the balcony and set it inside the poem,
and like the autumn morning sun the poem would flash a queen's smile.
Well, in my case, that's impossible—
no chance I can get away leaving a hot pot over the stove—
it makes me very angry but more than that, I feel sad
the time I pass with a heart full of pain and a mind full of rage
I can neither be a poet, nor a cook!
Unceasingly … unceasingly.

SHAMIM AZAD (b. 1952)

Changing Hands

I've been rowing icy oars, it's been really long
on my right the old field of compassion
someone has covered it with wax!
On my left, fragrant rice washed in soap water
and twelve kind of spices
being prepared for cooking up
a bat liver curry—
in front and behind me only
a river of male commentaries, where will I dock?

Ferrying my skeleton all over the place
I'm fatigued now.
So many murmuring Mahalayas[21] gone
even the goddess' untimely invocation passed
and in the swelling swathe of kaash flowers
I just became a photograph
never Durga herself.

In these unnatural locked down times
even amid a bumper crop of poetry all around
my fruits and grains are
outstanding and different,
that snow has heat inside

is not merely a woman's observation—
all sinners will know it as soon
as their skin burns down.

Enough rowing this icy boat; no more.
Let the premature fools take over now.

Honey Bee

I've turned into a honey bee sucking
the nectar of select people.
Now with this honey bee life-span
as long as I'm in this world
I'll keep stinging the arms of rascals.
In winter
till the time it takes for hundred flowers to bloom
till the stung miscreants do not
go raving mad
I'll keep buzzing around them
buzz…buzz…buzz,
then I'll quench my thirst,
while drinking my favourite flower-youth
I'll peep from the corridors of the creator to see
what a surprise!
Those stung people
are panicking at the sight of flowers
fearfully nursing their wounds.
Those vanquished men turn into flies
—flies cannot bite.

NASREEN NAIM (*b.* 1952)

Moving Time

Although my body is on fire at night
I don't see your face on waking up
I don't understand the singular logic
of living in such a pig pen.

This mortal relationship keeps jumping
like the koi fish put in ashes,
to douse the ambers, I pour a mug-full of water
in the potted mint sapling in my terrace.

Is there a province of desolation inside the mind?
But where shall I run away to, alas!
Instead of humans I have to listen to
wolves and jackals sing me lullabies.

The fire inside emboldens me
I want to break down the gates of false dreams
I want to fall asleep again to the song
of morphine before night strikes.

The Way of Earning

At that time there was no place for planting even one foot,
with a sweat-salted happiness
I set up on the silt banks of the Padma
a new chapter.
In the whirlpool of a jam-packed isolation
I keep searching for a wondrous brave touch
one that I've spotted among the teeming multitude,
in utmost reliance.

I keep it on my palm, in a lonesome blue solitude
within a soft silken caring,
I feel it.
I shoot an arrow at the thickened body of a tufted cloud
to have you.
Like the love of an ordinary undernourished youth
like the umbrella flying in the face of drought, flood, grief,
tearing wind, you're my hard-earned pride.

Today there's no painful crawling in my
staircase of climbing
because, I had earned the word freedom the day
I unbuttoned my chest.

DILARA HAFIZ (b. 1955)

I

Traversing through storms, great waves, and fires
here I am standing all by myself;
absolutely alone
no friends all this long except loneliness,
palm on palm,
to share the intimate pain with no holds barred.
Never had any companion to confide
in this very long journey as it winds up;
a cloud-capped sky mixed with a few words, phrases,
and rhythms has offered shade on my head.
Thunder and storms, snowfalls, volcanic eruptions
these are my constant companions,
I'm an ordinary girl child
my physical value is barely
more than mere zinc or copper.

I haven't forgotten…
Moments after my birth in the Age of Ignorance[22]
I used to be killed by strangulation
none in my paternal line
had ever been proud of me;
my brother weighs in gold even today
even in the waning days of his youth

he's still the pure gold meant for ornaments
the prime amulet to keep the bloodline secure—
I'm nobody, I do not exist anywhere
no stability whatsoever.
Yet after overcoming numerous storms, tides, and an apocalypse later
I am here today, alone, standing;

I know, more than ever,
I know that without me
this earth wouldn't move ahead even one step...
I'm that creator-spirit woman;
traversing storms, tidal waves, and fire
here I'm standing all alone—
a-l-l by myself.

ANJANA SAHA (*b.* 1955)

The Return

Unsolicited prayers gather
in the folds of sleepless nights.
I cannot look any longer
at your suffering-strained faced;
but as I keep staring I turn into stone
cross a fearsome bay and enter the nether worlds.
All of you who have offered on my lips
the graceful cup of hemlock
I take it to be the amrit[23], drink the nectar to the lees
I drown in the ethereal sea!
An insurmountable wave comes echoing
to snatch me down like the Titanic
pull me to the deep bottom of the ocean.
I struggle hard to escape.
Just like the cursed stone-Ahalya[24]
I keep building myself up
in stricken prayers;
my wounded pride I lay out
in all things soft and hard.
The way the reverberations of time's travels
keep coming back close to the earth,
within my own shadow I return thus.

The Curse

Why do I alone have to soak in
the sorrow-laden downpour of blue
dew drops every single day?
It is a relentless I who keeps pleading
at the feet of impossibility.
Why needlessly do you sow the seed of secret suspicion
in the private garden I tended with love and care?

So who's fault is it, really—
the blackened night's or mine?
In the hope of earning moksha[25]
at a penance like the stoic Ekalavya[26]
I hide away from everyone's sight.
You have no idea, fire, I know it
one can't buy with wealth anyone's deep sighs!

Wait till the lolling tongue of nature's revenge
plays the flute of apocalypse on your chest!

NURUNNAHAR SHIRIN (*b*. 1956)

Elegy for the Wind

And those newly tarred roads
that have started to get hot
the newly opened eyes
like the flowering jaba[27] in the garden
new words and sentences
the people's poems—
basically—all of what is new—
for all these things that gladden all hearts—
this silly head has dedicated
all forty-nine noons.
Early dawn memories of shiuli and bokul[28]
have calmed down her homeless nights.
Ah, on that sacrificed head she has gathered
dreams for the people—
infinite belief in blood—
everyone remembers in earnest—
those dawns are coming… they're coming…
new and red like the smell of memories of this life.

Equilibrium

The language of despondent days
who else have deciphered like burnt-out poets?
I mull, let the days ignore all fiery rage
let them find a picturesque equilibrium
the face that is deep inside the world of sensibility
the farthest off…
let it bloom.
Let it come and sit next to the shore of thirst.
Let it tell me each time that it
knows water's sound.
If under a cloud-smeared night it
opens its wounded toes forsaking footprints
to surge and gurgle in the water of poetry
let it float on the bottomless river-like love
and on the sharp peaks of a desire to see
if waves come and be spent,
let it weep in the fantastic land of six wonders.
And on seeing stains on roots, anchor,
let it absorb in blood an eternal debt…
let this seeing bring about the unseen light
in darkness, our face-to-face collective life.

Let There Be Some Anger

NASIMA SULTANA (1957-1997)

To You, Sorrow

Here, sorrow, I give you my bright handkerchief,
go back home, from today onwards we are eternally separated
I'll sit with three boyfriends today
will smoke in the dark
whiskey doesn't suit me,
a raging inferno burns my doubts
I have desire in my heart.
Very hot water and salt from the Bay of Bengal
then if a crow caws in the thick of noontime,
tell me, won't desire bend its head to the utmost low!
You are the sorrow of my not receiving any letter for over a month
you are the sorrow of my not writing poetry for over a month
you are the sorrow of my ambitions having been dead for over a month
today onwards it's eternal separation for us
I'm gifting you a bright handkerchief,
do return home
I'll sit in the darkness with three men friends and smoke a cigarette
without awakening the dead I'll snatch a cold breeze, the enigmatic evening
I'll say, ah how wonderful it is this staying alive!

Let There Be Some Anger

Let there be some anger thinking that the Peacock Throne[29] was ours one day
let something terrible happen.
It can't happen that each day suicidal thoughts come knocking at the door
each day the fragrant evening passes with ancient masks, wigs, belphool[30] garlands—
that cannot be the rule
each day life will drain away in failed lovemaking, it can't happen, it cannot!
Let there be some anger, let homes and hearths shake in extreme jealousy
and then in the moonlit field would descend hordes of men like wild animals
they'll tear asunder with their cruel claws all words of failure
and thus will slowly grow on their chest a crop of golden paddy
winter-harvest, the aroma of ilish[31], the pleasure of star fruits
on the sheetal-paati will awaken like jui[32] flowers a sweet smelling fist of rice.

Knowing once the Peacock Throne was ours, let's get angry
one day throwing off our robes under the sizzling sun, let everyone say
change our souls, O Lord
give us some anger.

SHAHJADI ANZUMAN ARA (*b.* 1958)

Doubt

Before pressing finger on the calling bell
I stop to think
am I the second one or the fifth?

The veil of doubt keeps hanging loose till my ankles
the lined up ants bite me hard
am I the first one or the third?

Wounded pride twists its waves within
with the stench of burnt leaves
deception swarms in rapidly
who knows if I'm the fourth one?

The dark ink of doubt flows on
my finger presses the calling button
the bell rings out on and on
the bird keeps on calling
as though a red hibiscus cloud will bloom in her throat.
First, second, third, or is it fourth, fifth?
The restless chandelier of time comes crashing down

I glance at the next door, alas,
all things accounted for here
a giant black bat hangs in there.

Coming to You

Why should I get up? It's my wish.
My wishes are forever awake
tuneful like a smooth flute, they make ripples in the wind
but I'm unhesitating.

In any blind closed hour,
I can easily rise whenever I please
holding dreams in my fist
stuff them in your hands
stealthily or in peopled precincts
that's hardly a bother
I come up without a dither.

The threshold of the closed door will weep and cry,
hiding my own dream in the hair's cascade of the dreamless,
like the light, suddenly piercing blinding darkness
I'll come up, I can come for you
at any time

Now it's an interlude to rise and come.

JHARNA RAHMAN (b. 1959)

From the Heart of Words

I'm not an astronomer
have never peeked through a telescope ever
although my walls are ancient
the whitewash is patchy and long fallen in chunks
still in any of its secret nooks there was no
astronomical booklet or design printed on thin tree barks

But I knew for sure
one day on a blazing star there would be a massive explosion
a terrible sound would pervade the infinite universe,
from the smoke of the void will fly
many skies layer by layer
and on that will slowly take shape the impression of your face.

I had been through villages and hamlets
on uneven rough dirt roads
walking straight down—there was in my eyes
like a green fruit turning juicy
the jingle of a well-strung instrument from the song of reckless youth,
the fearsome five star-studded sword at Kalpurush's[33] waist
I've been holding on to firmly with my five fingers.
Along the long road I traversed droplets of blood saga
trickling down. The earth had turned red.

As though the eternal potter was thrusting hands inside the flaming oven
to take out, like hot molten lava,
sharp enchanted earthen word art forms.

Words rally behind me
words scream and rush out of the grains of crops
words splutter milk, bursting and sprinkling out of paddy spikes
even then from the sawing sound of logged fruit trees
the pungent smell of the raw sap float around—
through all of these sound-smell-touch
hearing your sound, smelling your form
lost in the ecstasy of your embrace I walk on.

Woman

The smell of woman inside the night a sleeping woman awake inside her sari inside the sari the smell of woman the two-step woman a halved right angle

A definitive geometry the woman after nightfall gets divided among five husbands Draupadi[34] to die in Dushshashan's[35] hand when her endless sari is not to be found

In blood and flesh the fire of skin an enchanting smoke of half-burnt stench within honey breaks the honeycomb in heady primitive copulation rites

Inside leaves in the milk of grains the smell of woman sprinkles green inside the earth piercing the seed base rises a fertile tower of crops

Inside night the smell of woman in sandalwood grove a burning woman tree inside trees fragrant firewood a dance of chandan[36]-pyre in salt water waves.

TASLIMA NASRIN (b. 1962)

Emancipation

Forget, if you want to forget.
Don't pester me suddenly time to time on mobile, emails, sitting far apart.
Sitting far apart don't annoy me by pelting your frozen silence.

If you forget I'll at least know you have forgotten,
if you forget I'll kick off my toe-pinching shoes and walk barefoot for a while,
if you forget I'll shed off all the attire of expectation and take a bath,
if you forget I'll again play the old songs,
if you forget I'll open all the windows and sleep carelessly the way I please.
Let sunshine or moonlight come play hide and seek in my body, I'll just sleep,

It's been long I wanted so much to sleep in peace but couldn't sleep at all!
Spent time in waiting. Spent in sleeplessness. Kept standing at the window.

There's someone who remembers me, wants me ardently, the whole of me,
someone who'd knock at my door any time whether day or night,
then I have to face him as flawless, as though my hair, as though face, as though eyes, lips,
as though breasts, my chin, birthed right now, nowhere broken, unscratched, untouched by dust.
I'm expected to smile like the princess in a fairy tale,
in case he feels hungry and thirsts for a cup of tea
everything should be at hand flawless!

I have to love flawless!
I should be immersed in him flawless!
I must appear small and that too flawless!
How long have I fooled myself, have been calling nightmare by the name of bliss!

Do forget if you want to forget, such a relief.
More you want to remember me, more you want me, more you want to get close,
more you say 'love me', more I'll be a prisoner in your heart, a prey in your net,
trampled under your feet, locked in your clenched fist, your claws on me.

Do forget, I'll wash the paint off my face and feel a bit lighter, feel a bit me.

Love

If I have to wear kajal in my eyes for you,
have to paint my face and hair,
have to perfume my body,
have to wear my best sari for you,
because only you'll appreciate I have to wear a necklace, bangles
if the fatty layer of my tummy,
if the crease on my neck or at my eyes' corner have to be carefully hidden,
then we have something else, it's not love with you.

If it is love, then whatever is my careless disorder
whatever defects, whatever the mistakes, let it be ugly,

I'll stand before you, you will love.

RAHIMA AKHTER KALPANA (*b.* 1962)

Ten Haiku

1.
early morning
little snails
   drink dew drops

2.
migrant bird's flight
like the hunter's arrow
   clouds turn red

3.
in the dead of night
silence gets sawed
   by a voice

4.
merry chatter sounds
candles light up party hall
   I burn alone

5.
on the sea shore
spread out a long beach
   home is here

6.
little jasmine blossoms
in children's mouth
   two tiny teeth

7.
unknown flower
blooms even in neglect
   in matchless glow

8.
split wooden logs
sawed down trees
   the market is nigh

9.
slow-moving snail
travels a long way
   there's no looking back

10.
this black waterfall
the night sleeps
   in my beloved's hair

Price Quote

The sorrows will be all auctioned, all of them
come buy them, I'll sell them all at your price
all of them.

All the pain arranged together I write leaf by leaf
my peace of mind gone, in the blue book of hurt
leaf by leaf

My dreams will be all dead, graves in shrouds
if you hear the news, bring your eyes full of sky
to graves in shrouds

I found no place in your heart, nor in water
walking alone in storms and winds, lonesome din
no place in water

The sorrows will be all auctioned, all to buy
come get them, I'll sell them at your quoted price.

FERDOUS NAHAR (*b.* 1962)

Translated Reflections

That old railroad
near the water every time, I remember it all
the sky has dropped its serene blue eyes in the water, keeps sitting;
you had run along the rail line because someone
was arriving. Being topsy-turvy with emotion is this I suppose.

That spring, while looking at the green trees, the red-feathered
exiled birds that flew away to the Andaman had said—
everything is deceit! The shadow of water laughs, from laughter an illusion,
from illusion emerges an unknown silence; sound of whistle floats in

The translated reflections reiterate, do check once more
if you left anything behind in this desolate waiting room.

Autumn of the North

In my sleep I hear the song of falling leaves
yard after yard the leaves lay strewn, I crackle
them under my feet, remember from a concert
Begum Akhtar's voice ring out loud in a song—
she'll sing the unfulfilled azaan[37] of a pre-winter autumn

Once I part the rusted gate, a riot of colours greets me
a voice calls like a friend, in a clear deep assuring tone
while I leave, the imbued meaning of that ardent call
in autumn's breath creates colours all over High Park
to Fuller Road, where deep hues change my breath

The leaves swirl around in rage, in the autumn of the north
rings out unseen smells, drawn towards an anxious pull

Who goes, whoever goes spellbound in the taint of east wind;
since I don't know, the end of sunset's play in unknown dark
paints a flying autumn on an inscribed note.

Debt of Words

It's been so long I'm returning home at midnight
as I pass near your home
the days of our forgotten antaras[38] flash a smile

Summer-lust bustle, calling out names the soft night wind
had touched the waiting courtesan's cat on a wide Tashkent road
even today customers in black cars come pick up cat-women in dark
matryoshkas[39] on shop shelves had been singing in a chorus even then

All of those songs so heart-rending.

BILORA CHOWDHURY (b. 1966)

Love

1.
How can the blue breeze even dare
to extinguish this magic candle!
It has kept hidden
the pride of its wick
inside an intoxicated
drunk mirror.

2.
I'm measuring my void
along the longitude of your distance.
As much fallen leaves
as lonesome feathers
as many silk cocoons
on blueish wings
as silken separations;
my nemesis pierced
on your fleeting fragrance…

3.
His half-shadow
etched on half-darkness.
The offshoots of branches have

burst into a leafy delirium.
Even then their wordiness stays hidden
quietly like the old salt-stricken wall.
Pitter-patter falls rain water
leaf moves, inside leaves!

4.
Waterfalls in flight
now they've turned into mist.
You're plucking the mist-vapour flowers
to adorn my hair bun,
like a homebound river
along your banks
I'm flowing on secretly.

The Chanting

What is this pitcher of nectar on the chandelier!
It keeps ringing, upturned in its self-centredness:
within the otherworldly now the worldly is released
put my flame out, put me out, put me out.

In the blood still whips on the intoxication of neem[40]
in the garden hangs Orpheus' pain
what is this spark inside a ball of fire!
How do I forget, the heaven rocks.

On earth has descended a glacial circumference
the quicksilver has not yet reached its heated moment
the stoic sky is showing its palm of abhaya[41]
what is this undulation of grass in the quietened blood!

SHAHNAZ NASREEN (*b.* 1967)

Mind in Flight

Go on keep vigil but the mind will take flight
hearing the grass call it'll soar away to Brindaban[42]
on return it'll spin for you a beautiful fairy tale

This way in order to hide nail marks
and hair shed on pillow cases
stories would generate—hundreds and thousands of them
word seeds such as cats, thorny bushes, pesky kids
colourful keywords for these tales

And the manuscripts would get smuggled out
in the pantry, pond sides, or someplace more inaccessible
to keep life's attire all ironed and spiffy—
these tales sell well in our society.

My Younger Brother

My younger brother, we are close in age
our birth months on alternate years
one day the entire house is struck by mourning
people diving into the pond, great commotion
that day my brother died from drowning

From that day on, this loneliness is so sharp
everything is lonesome,
laying quietly in the lap of night
clutching the bolster in a strange fear
calling it brother, my brother

Leaving all chores, mother is bedridden
father has turned away his face in failed hatred
many others keep saying
oh no, the girl lives, it's the boy who's gone

I keep roaming around the house
for a few ounces of compassion
if face to face with father his eyes burn me through
he gets enraged I could even dare be alive
in curse after curse he perhaps wishes for my end
I still keep growing up uncared untutored
in my breast I hide the blazing iron of a smithy
I keep growing up, I grow

The news headlines claim
a brutal father has thrown acid on his girl child
my father seems to me a great soul.

KOCHI REZA (b. 1968)

Locked Down

I wake up early, don't let the dawn slip, I see
how deserted is the road out there. I see a car or two and a rickshaw on the main road.
Rabindranath playing in my room. In my lonely room.
"Which broken path did you traverse in the sleepy night
Whatever belonged to mine that broke became blessed at your feet."
The neem sapling roots in the pot all dried up. And these fragrance-less flowering plants.
One cactus growing defiant. All of them need water.
Cloudless sky. Day without rain or storm. Time is the enemy!
I don't climb down the stairs. Is death on the staircase, at the gate when I step out?
A few pigeons still fly. They drink water on their beaks from the AC ducts.
Is everything okay? I can walk down. Could I go as far as I desired?
Could I move through the crowd in the bazaars, pushing out their elbows?
Quo vadis[43], earth, to which path of destruction?
Is this the strawberry-coloured world I had?
I keep looking at my potted plants. Now I understand their silence!
I understand all that conversation between bark and leaves, stem and the breeze.
Perhaps they've spoken to me as well. I didn't hear. Now I do.
A neem-like tree keeps calling all day long.
I water her at crack of dawn, the roots are thirsty I realize.
When after bath I go to the verandah to hang my clothes to dry,
the tree speaks up exactly in a neem-voice,
Give me water, Ma. A little water.

Bijita, Does Your Cousin Touch Your Breasts?

Today I feel like calling out, Bijita, Bijita
Bijita a name from childhood
Bijita, Bijita, go to school, eat butter on steaming rice
Teacher is here, don't go to play now Bijita
Bijita, listen to your elders
Bijita, you'll grow up to be Indira Gandhi
Bijita, life is a smudge
Then?
Bijita, wash your face thrice everyday with soap
Bijita, be humble, don't laugh out loud
Sit with your harmonium
Don't study inside the room alone with a male tutor
If boyfriends write letters pass them on to your mother
Bijita, Bijita, make sure your orna[44] is in place!
Bijita, does your cousin touch your breasts?
Don't hide anything
I don't hide anything, Ma!

LEESA GAZI (*b.* 1969)

Forever Fragrance

Yesterday's words are bygones
the words reverberate, but meanings are bygones
sentences are still expressive, utterances are bygones
didn't you just say, no? We'll forget tomorrow itself
grass, leaves, flowers that we will touch, and forget all
only forever fragrance.

Clouds want to steal a look at you, hence dew-cradled
although the world is miserly, desire is migratory
once the light comes emitted by the dark itself
this mind of clay doesn't store anything at all.
Other than your wonder it doesn't remember a thing
you just looked back, no? I'll forget tomorrow itself
only aggression will stay in mind
whether this evening falls or not
yet forever fragrance.

Yesterday's words are bygones
the words reverberate, but meanings are bygones
sentences are still expressive, utterances are bygones
you just uttered, no? We'll forget tomorrow itself
grass, leaves, flowers that we will touch, and forget all
only forever fragrance.
Whether this evening falls or not
yet forever fragrance.

The Chase

It doesn't help to look backwards while walking
the moment you look back, images assault your mind's mirror
unruly breeze grime and sweat, the din and whistle of the train
plaintive cry of a thirsty dog, on bird's wings the afternoon's stealth
all of these go around, go round and round

It doesn't help to look backwards while walking
the moment you do there's blood from stumbling against a rock
the grey morning wishing for sunlight
in the turns of the era of kali[45], the dearth of time
all of this happens, they keep happening
in love and care in storms in conflicts
all of this takes place every day, they keep happening

SHAHNAZ MUNNI (b. 1969)

White Void

The deep love will remain unrequited
and you'll run away to Mathura or Uranus fearing scandal
the spate of my endless tears have flowed in to the Yamuna or Thames
you must still know I've saved the memory of all those kisses on my lips,
an illusory demon lives across the blue door
there's blood stains on his discarded shoes, the stink of puke,
your terrible contaminating force
is blowing a sand storm, the earth is sinking, don't you feel
the life I've arrived at defying the deathly pull of breathlessness,
it is all dusty, like darkness amid a twister, don't you realize…

O melancholic muddy road will you take me home
I'm burning to turn into a lamp, an upwards climbing staircase is calling
two doves lament in a plaintive tone
in the obscured dusk
I'm lying on the road like a dry sprig of straw
the wind knows I'm flying inside a white void.

Immobile Pendulum

No mangrove in the world can prevent this salty flood
happiness, laughter, and loves of humans will now be salt-stricken
in the same whirlpool, dancing dolphins will repeatedly lose their way
our ship has got lost in the sea of smoke in search of pure freedom
although the ocean disagreed, although the sky wore a melancholy mendicant's garb
and there was thundering sound, in teeth and tongue the roar of waves

Since you cannot hold your immobile heart still
you remain unknown everywhere
you remain free, minus the burden of memory
far away from the past, present or future breathing down on you
you remain sleepless, in thrall of dreams

Only my shadow follows your shadow
as though it isn't a shadow but a flying moth,
like a three-legged cowherd boy chasing his cow
like it was slippery sunlight on the verandah,
like the sense of a deep darkness which has no explanation
or an unresolved puzzle recited by my grandmother

I understand all of that after many many days

SHELLY NAZ (b. 1969)

Enigma

A gusty river below my waist, blue whales' song
I have pierced with a golden spear kept eternally along

This is all for you, all fireworks, flower-lakes, stealth
of riptides in my breasts, grapes of wrath

Dig up the ashes of the lampstand and see, a star burns softly
you fill your pockets and depart to a forest of mystery

I've flown away the balloons filled with my breath that sing
I unhooked safety pins to let sari folds tumble out in the spring

Wheat fields that wail aloud at your curved knife of battle
the steam and poison that has poured out of the steaming kettle

They're all dissatisfied, yet for you I keep aside veins full of wine
if not in mine, then let in your pleasure cruise celebrations begin

I serve you milk, fresh blood, in the finest China bowl
O utmost enigma, my man, even then your indifference, your scowl!

Fallen from Heaven

Silk in your fingers, sleep on a tour of the body, thirst a pilgrim,
I'm gathering water, small and massive waves of lusty nights

Swallows bathing naked, a tumbler full of tiny fire on the skin of ice
heavy breathing in the blouse, a chiffon river in the sari, hands magnet

Thirst begins at lips, in the desert of tongue, in the white underbelly of sea
this is a false dam of sands, the thousand-wheel speed of the sluice gate

Keeps increasing in length and breadth in a roar, I'm playing a sitar[46]
breathless in the street's song. In the garden a skeletal tree, stars full of leaves

Fearful attendant, unfaithful slave this thirst of mine
eyes made of clouds, an ashadh[47] gone headless, rife with metal smells

I'm waiting for the match stick to kiss the half-lit cigar
the way a red wine-filled glass waits for the touch of lonely lips

What use is heaven to me where the man enjoys thousand apsara[48]s
on my velvet couch I want your strong arms of a seasoned jeweller!

NAHAR MONICA (*b.* 1969)

The Tale of Tunes

We had a dozen or so playmates in our close neighbourhood
where there was no sea, the shadow of sea came and sickened the nights.
Once such nights deepened, gathering the tunes churning in their pores
the girls would run out in high noon,
the hunter breeze would chase them down straight to the rail lines.
The girls have long played on the rail lines as though on harmonium reeds
they've played upon each other, each other's rib cage.

Our neighbourhood homes had no harmonium,
only a few song-feathers,
they catch the tunes with perfect rhythm, go speeding on the train
the girls would sing aloud, practice the notes along with the rhythm of relationship.
From the start to the end, the inevitable udaara and mudaara
play on perfectly till the flowers of taar saptak[49] blossom in the misty dawn.

Back then the mist still gave us the colour blue, the birds…
as the river flowing along the octaves stooped at their sombre feet,
the light in the girls' eyes spread its wings tipsy with the half-blinking stars…
or let me say it this way, the way the entire childhood these girls,
knee-deep in waves, singing full throated, wanted to turn into conch shells,
to play on in the endless water wrapt in tune with them.

Other than the sea shore, conch shells do not see good climes—

not a single intoxicated one came breaking nature's codes
to sleep like a sloth in our ancient neighbourhood,
now since time has waned there's none to play the whistling tune—
who'll teach the girls the taste of a booming conch!
So the girls fly away alone on their own tunes
their breasts bearing little roots of wings, shooting upwards.

The Garden of Eve

The evening moon becomes the escort to some ashen nights
is that even possible?
Hesitating with little-known pleasure, tree leaves perform new conjugal rites.
Near the shadow of leaves, humans in darkness, that is I and the man
nurturing the stitches of wound inside our palms we pick and eat poems in silence,
hanging fruits falling down from our arms,

we want to take an able oath by the young light.

The meaning is happy once wiped out of the word's meaning—

Liquorice blows in the wind by thoroughfares, heels cautious on fallen leaves' sound.
Searching for futile pleasure my man chases the aaheli[50] beetle,
leafy tree-vine burns alone, it moves to the Ishaan[51] direction all charred—
we demur, then write out in music the saga of our solitary life.

Unhooking the anchor of shade the careless dusk moon wears its light on ankles
come morning the leaves forget their night-time rhythm and art.
Still more is left to talk in the courtyard of dawn—
Who can swing more? Or us, meaning I and the man
stay in the thrall of darkness, day and night hungry for shadows we live.
We swing in the happiness of leaves, some sorrow left to swing in the day's business.
Moon the companion has recognized our wet footsteps, she has spread
the news to youthful leaves.

AYSA JHORNA (*b.* 1969)

Chastity

I crumple up and hide among innumerable people, limbs folded.
This one comes, that one comes, gauges out my eyes; eyeless
eye hole oozes blood. Someone comes and tears out
my nose ring, while they look for the nose ring.
Someone comes looking for my nose ring
and ends up tearing it apart.

Someone probes my chastity; someone for the shankha-sindoor[52].
They scalp me while looking for sindoor.
They break my bangles and my bones protrude.
I'm still a stone; a dot crumpled and folded up
stabbed many a times, my mother cushions me on her breasts.
She says, 'Daughter come to me, I will take
you again in my womb.' Just then I wake up
from my stone-slumber, sleep in peace against my mother's chest.
To ease my death she sings me a lullaby,
which spreads in the crystal clear river-stream. Where
droplets of blood fall relentlessly from a tree called death.

Maple Leaf

There's a storm raging, there's a latent fear in this city spreading
like a virus, it's called death. At any time death can snap
your neck you wouldn't even know. You only think, will death
be painless or terrible!
Those that are dead, if they returned to tell how much tolerable it was
at the time of dying. You roam around in hidden fear, see kaashphul[53]
blooming. See how blue is the autumn sky.

Devi's[54] invocation, Buddha's ahimsa[55] sermons, Jesus in his merciful mien,
none of these can calm us down.
You think you'll leave and go away to be safe from this death-scare.
Where will you go, everywhere lies in wait the dilemma of trust and mistrust.
You are enamoured seeing a maple leaf, you sing maple leaf
maple leaf, you don't know it'll snow just in a few days,
all of that beauty would be gone with winter lashing in.

What's a Woman Gotta Do in Heaven

SHANTA MARIA (b. 1970)

What's a Woman Gotta Do in Heaven

Heaven has no poet
so what's a woman gotta do in Heaven.

Wide-eyed hoors[56]
keep dancing nonstop
along the corridors of Heaven.

No lovers in Heaven
no enchanting flirtations
the ambiance of Heaven? Quite boring
spic and span, all severely arranged in a neat row.

Where's forest in Heaven?
Sea or rivers?
Mandakini, Al-Kawthar, Lethe?
If it doesn't meander wild
breaking banks in frenzied ecstasy
how is it even a river?

In the Heaven-corridor you see pious men and women
praying day and night
no desire or lust in Heaven
aspiration or disappointment

sorrow and all that enticing tamasha[57]
where are the wild reckless men
in the heart of Heaven?
Neither there's death written anywhere—
what's a woman gotta do in Heaven anyway.

Personal Night of Moonlight Gathering

Then we drowned neck deep in the moonlight's sharaab[58]. Little by little the blue intoxication seeped inside our being. The jamdaani[59] darkness embroidered with starry patterns. All over our body a rousing lunar festival. The ancient moon god on emerging from the churning of the sea opened up for us a hamper full of gems. And all of us stark lonely people discarded our clothes of silence to mingle together under one single cover of the night. I didn't see your eyes, neither had you seen mine. That night we were hypnotized by our own sights. The spider moon was about to swallow us in its threads of light. There was no death on that night. Or perhaps we had stolen sleep from the eyes of the dead. If we seem dead to each other, any night born of the moon would revive us. Even in the frozen darkness of a seamless death in a growing lunar phase, whether in oblivion or remembrance, we would again be rejuvenated. On that strange night Selene and Endymion came to life and taught us how to love. And let me confess in private, whenever I wish to bathe within you, I return bringing back a piece of moonlight from that precious night of yore.

MEGH ADITI (b. 1970)

Droplets of Memory

I've given you all that is deep within me
the kingfisher eye of my navel, private haritaki[60] groves
still you look for droplets of memory, when secretly in the closet
I guard my heart in meaningless boundless sorrow
I keep myself aside thinking this hide-and-seek is fun
I'll remain in this journey in tattered multiplication tables
this is not you, who I know to be the unbound one

In which level of consciousness does love reveal itself?
Unknown is the answer, hence I'm that hunted target
what you call love is what I know as touch …

Jhaaptaal

In the common valley of the bedsheet
a matryoshka has placed its face

In the squared light there

One, two, three ... glass smithereens
I pick them up and think
if you keep talking about cure
my gesture is towards healing
scarred in hundred places
watchfully being diminished into invisibility I feel
this time I will learn the jhaaptaal[61] beats

Let a bridge stay awake
in the depth of this midnight...

Poet

From tree-lined homes to a wondrous solitude
the breeze piercing through the navel of isolation has stopped,
only that person who alone
has touched the chin of her beautiful mistake
only that person who alone
has kept her touch safe from fire

From the din of words to the farthest grief
calling out repeatedly in seclusion
she has slept off at last
desiring a kiss, that poet

A moon rolls down from her pen
on the paper her half-burnt life.

MONIKA CHAKRABORTY (b. 1971)

Zero Sum Game

1.

I was completely my own.
Independent. Free-willed.
Yet last night all over my bed there was—a different kind of charm.
My whole body still—waiting for you—
for the first time I pondered—all the colourful shirts in the stores
have been stitched only for your wear—
while speaking you sometimes touch the side of your chest—
in that wide plain—invisible
to eyes I sow—
my deep, intense roots.

2.

I felt melancholy, at midnight, in half-awakening
the tunes of sadness turning even sadder to blow away—
the burden of this failed life.
Sky full of moon beams, our stony love
carries along joy and death—
in a Moonlight Sonata.

3.

The mountain top seems to be melting—
in the depth of a white mist.
But you may think,
this wondrous evening is short-lived—
the dawn sunlight will draw in the yellow-redness of jealousy.
I try to save time from slipping away, in the cloak of trust, stealthily
in meagre, lifeless hope—
the other side of envy, the greenery of crops.

4.

As long as I can gaze at time—I do
inside the hidden gusto of photo albums.
In those pictures of marital bliss—
the fragrance of a condensed past—
two moons in a close encounter.
Face to face with a specific photograph—I stand.
My face is like Ophelia—hands and legs tied—
I'm drowning.
And your eyes are watching that spectacle—
the eyes of an unmoved, black cat.

5.

If you attempt to write poetry
you'll learn to stand—
alone with your shadow.
Can't even trust the shadow, she too is a fugitive.
She'll leave you alone, or will lead you—
to your own skeleton.
Over there a new beginning and a ritual of shava-sadhana[62]—
through the emerging waves, a zero-sum game.

ALAKA NANDITA (*b.* 1971)

White Saris

Let white kaash flowers float on the river
let the autumn clouds go merge within the blues
on soft cold nights heavenwards

    I've blown away my mother's white saris;

let the home in mourning wear dazzling lights
let fireflies dim in that splendour
so that departed souls don't come crowding in the flower garden

    charmed by the desolate blue grass;

those that believe in clowning to keep us happy
make us sad once they are afar
for them fireflies stay up kaash blossoms float on

    clouds roam about with the watchful kite;

now I won't pay heed to anyone
draw a chalk circle of my own
I'll set on fire the white saris of my mother

    stealthily on one full moon night.

Revenge

So many are happy that the paths to my return are closed
you too are one of them. Leaving me here,
the home where you peer in, she's married too I know
one by one everyone will know
the intimate stories of our household
I'm thinking, I'll buy you a mirror
all alone every day you'll see your reflection
your arrogant face,
while walking along the path of collaborators
you too will get drenched in a torrential rain—
then will I be cured
of my own malady.
Is nothing more … or less.

Eye Glasses

Once upon a time the path for all six of us was one.
Our joy and pain would be expressed in one language.
While walking we used to think
why doesn't the road get longer.

In the wild breeze of our vagabond lives
we'd become indispensable for each other.
To those struck by jealousy we appeared as bigwigs.

Our secret chats would slip through our fingers
to mingle in faraway villages where arhar[63] fields stretched,
by the thin river's bend
the kingfisher would perch waiting.

Everything afar was very clear to us then.
Now I can hardly see without my eye glasses.

FARHANA RAHMAN (b. 1972)

Tale of Autumn

Did the faraway sea want to tell
a new story?
But my legs had got stuck in
self-immersed water…
because autumn has struck the season
I've carelessly left the hem of my earthy clothes to trail
because I've become moonstruck,
in the time of inferno
mingled in the hot summer wind
flowers from even leafless trees
seem to appear as stars of night.

The lute of passion strums in the incense-scented breeze
in the empty palms of the frigid earth
snow-memory in the heart brings forth
the illusion of sanyas[64].

Walking far very far to arrive under
a deep shadow
humans merely leave
their own real selves …

Kojagori Awakening

Away from my daily life
to watch leaves fall one by one
from the body of trees
I leave deep forests to go stand atop a hill.
Enveloped by the enchantment of a naked silence
the lonesome primitive moon is getting drenched
touched by the kojagori[65] full moon,
in the lunar horizon shadows swing capped in emptiness
unbelievably beautiful all around—
perhaps autumn has been unravelled only in the forest.
I'm reminded of so much
so much unexpected negligence
dove's cry
indolent aches on phases and days
unseen roar of laughter, melody of flutes
churning of distant memory in impermanent ties!
Still why's there so much thirst in the body and mind?
I know there aren't any answers to these questions
thus a few of us carry amazement in our eyes
after our lonely sojourn is done
we get lonelier
and watch only ourselves from afar!

JUNAN NASHIT (*b.* 1973)

Black Poison

Eyes pierced by the knife's blade
fiery waves coursing through the bones
a helmet of waiting adorned across the invisible forehead

Before the eyeballs sink inside wordless weeping
I take off the helmet of waiting and go for a spin
to the brink of that moment where life was lost,
the spot where one day I touched your shoulders, blew
swathes of breeze, locked our lips, the palm of our tongues.

The tune you play today in every aggression
it carries the stark draught of damage, a black poison.

Both eyes on dagger's edge
blood-flow of longing keeps trickling along the nostrils.

Neanderthal's Grave

Life is supine
in an invisible Neanderthal's grave!

A mad rush at the head of the deceased
vociferous mallika petals, siren wails, commotion—
seeing this the woodpecker's slumber is broken
he too tramples on his wish-bells and raises a tune
the sign-sound whistling from a pre-palaeolithic era—

It's a sad tune!
Hence the resounding void churns a vortex in fire-filled eyes!

At the end of a bone-charring day
the airless house unshackles the hands of the grave—
the windows of the home and a speechless expanse outdoors.
I try to train my ears from many krosh[66] away
I don't hear a thing
because there's no weeping in that house
no tremulous sighs even by mistake
there are leaf attires all in a row
they come up all over me, on my face
they spread a strange delirious babble all over my body
as though they're the unguarded frost of a glass-chimney sand-clock
an odd-hour violin strain.

The day our accumulated anger wipes out this civilisation
life chokes
beyond the chimney smokes it also looks for
in the cave art of Altamira[67]
a vast water body in a spontaneous flow.

NAHIDA ASHRAFI (*b.* 1973)

Our Mother was a Fool

We knew our mother was very poor. But we three siblings hardly cared about that. No truth is greater than food to starved bellies. So when hungry, I used to scream even louder than the trumpet sound made by angel Israfil[68], and rent the air and sky.

Our mother would then take out from an earthen pot some wheat flour of history to mix it with a dollop of geography and make us rotis. On the scalding skillet the flatbread would start to resemble an endangered map.

That day we got to know how sound a historian our mother was.

We can't swallow the roti all dry. Mother said, 'Smear some lies on it, my pets. Lies work like butter. And it makes swallowing the roti easier too.'

That day it dawned on us what an ace politician our mother was.

We had no manoeuvring skill in the society, no roof overhead, no rice on the stove—chaal[69]. We cared little for the first two. But for cooked rice we could put our hands inside a wolf's mouth or even in a snake's hole. Although all of these weren't necessary. Mother knew exactly where the rat holes were in the paddy fields. The whole day's collection is only three fistful of rice. How much water need be added to make sure we three get starchy rice for the day's two meals, our mother measured correctly.

That day we realised what an expert mathematician our mother was.

Epitaph

I couldn't arrange for green grass in the garden of my heart for the beli[70] and bokul to shed on. I couldn't tell the gondhoraj[71] this garden is yours. You can bloom in peace. I couldn't have a pool for the lotus. I never at all had the ability to buy a soulful night that I could gift the hasnahana[72]. To have the ducks dive in freely all day, I couldn't get a pond with the play of sun and shade. The laburnum and myrtle had wanted to chat on a spread made out of water. The koel's esraaj[73] playing its fine notes in the background. Where will I ever get such an expensive afternoon?

Please forgive me shiuli, lotus, myrtle, laburnum. Do forgive me, gondhoraj, hasnahana. Forgive me, soulful nights, sleepy afternoons, mossy banks of green ponds.

One morning of hemanta[74], thousands of dew-soaked shiuli will lie scattered on the grave of this green lover of yours. You do know, the grass on the grave in hemanta is always strikingly green.

AUDITY FALGUNI (*b.* 1974)

Plague Plays a Holi

These stars and planet clusters all night long
mighty comets cruising around
they're sending us waves of God-particle,
our mute garrulousness all day and night,
our garden parties, gossip and whispers
brilliant light dazzles down from stars and plant clusters!
In this time of plague
in this era of viral contagion
the God-particles that rain down from the multitude of stars,
the way paint drops scatter from your brush,
and the droplets from your brush stroke
the endless colours
redden my cheeks,
both my hands, forehead, and hair
so unknowingly, so quietly?
But Dol[75] isn't allowed during Corona!
Holi[76] is banned
still an endless acrylic colour
has drenched my scarf-skirt-veil …
Hey there, cruel artist!
Don't you know no festival of colours in Corona?
No colour splashing out of squirt guns?
No colour powder smearing on cheeks and forehead?

Why so cruel O Kanhaiya[77]!
In the time of contamination today
no people and revellers on Yamuna banks
even Radha is in quarantine,
and you still playing with colours all alone?
Braja gopis[78] play Hori...
Please go back, Kanhaiya!
Do not attempt to smear colours on me
please no infection for me! I want to remain
innocent, pure and well protected ...
colourless and untouched,
the way I have been all these while!

RAHIMA AFROOZ MUNNI (*b.* 1974)

Modesty

This puny form of mine covered in skin
I want to emerge out of this sheathe,
break out of the secret cabin of the tongue that keeps getting arrested
skip the surveillance of forever frightened eyes,
behind me the call for bisarjan[79] in water.

This awkward soul gathered in tattered pity like a beggar,
even after following all the civilised norms and rules
is not able to fit itself at all under this straightjacket,
unsavoury habits causing it to decay and fester...
The habits that dangle like thunder's sharp cue,
the haha roaring laughter that chills the bones,
the morgue where stuffy days and nights merge together,
bit by bit I'm leaving these behind emerging ahead...

What otherworldly warmth is this, spreading over
the folds of my body seeping into the blood—as though
the stormy red day has arrived with great zeal.
This day on—I'm tearing off the cover of modesty,
I just cannot hide myself away any more.

The Wild

Turn your face towards us,
the earth is meant for us too,
even we're featured in imaginations through epochs,
within our ancestors' memories,
within the securities of your future.

Now we want to die in this forest itself
with the remaining autumnal leaves going to rest.
Molten lead will cover us all over
our stories of solidarity entwined in wild vines.

Do feel it,
the joy of pouring suffering in us.

Do touch,
we're beautiful luxury items once skinned alive.

NOVERA HOSSAIN (*b.* 1975)

Existentialism

No cooking gas the whole day
sundry items lying in the oven, on the stove top
pop out the fridge basket and the smell of plagued dead rats hits you —
a sudden flock of wild geese takes flight towards the kitchen;

Corridor, stair-well
no light anywhere
it's a black-out throughout the night

Yet you say
now there's plenty of water in the river Nile

No one will sleep
mortar shells keep piercing the night

You sit and think
someone will find you too;

No one is around anywhere today
was never there;

mortar shells all night long
stench of gunpowder
sparks of light

Torn Clouds

Rows of fragrance-less potted flowers on the rooftop
pollen grains are agape at the jaba's high-pitched voice
people are stepping in fear in cautious calculation
mouths hidden behind masks
thirsting at the downpour of srabon[80]
even then they stay at three arms-length distance from each other
voices traveling across the wire wear out thin
no one is on the other side
still you plant your ears to hear
the bellowing of a conch
somewhere salt waves crashing
torn clouds in the sky
bits of torn love in the ether
they retreat when you want to touch them
bird feathers scattered across the courtyard

JAHANARA PERVEEN (b. 1975)

The Song of Spices

There's no God inside my fist
there was an ant; but it left

The green marble that I had
from my dadi[81]'s trunk
it was there for a while
it also knows that enchantment is the mother of regret

A cardamom pod had told me—
she doesn't like spice groves
she wants to have a fist-clutched life

I fill up the glass jar
with fistful of cardamom wishes.

Crime

A two-storied house on a little strip of a verandah;
south wind blowing to and fro into the house
and flitting sparrows

Ma used to hunt the sparrows, their family and fledglings
      to satisfy the hunger that camped in our kitchen

Doors, windows, all ventilators shut
birds flitting helter-skelter, screeching in fear
      I still remember my mother's cruelty

On her children's plates my Ma would serve
breast, wings, liver of the bird mother,
whose babies waited for her
in the tree nearby

I ask for forgiveness from the sparrow perched on the grill
      for the crimes my mother committed

SHAKIRA PARVIN (b. 1977)

Tree Bulletin

1.

The entire tree has fallen asleep. One leaf is awake. The tree wakes up in the midnight.
She can feel the leaf sighing. She tells the leaf, sleep now. I will sing to you.
She fans the leaf in a murmur with her twigs and branches and other leaves.
The leaf home fills up with dew drops.

2.

The tree has kept safely with itself a sindoor[82] casket. A long time has passed since.
How much longer will she hide storms, rains, fires, thinks the tree.
Then one day a woodcutter comes and sits under her shade. He holds a sharp axe.
On an impulse she drops the sindoor casket. It lands on his lap.
Sindoor box in hand the woodcutter keeps wondering.
Then he takes a fistful of sindoor and daubs it endearingly on the tree's forehead.
Her tree-life is blessed.

3.

That leaf used to always pray… let spring season not come at all.
The tree prayed may it come.

It's best if spring came.
The old would fall. The new would sprout.
One time the leaves took out a protest against springtime.
No flowers bloomed that time. No birds sang.

Accusation

I haven't been able to write ever since I became a poet.
I'll murder those that have made me a poet.

They stayed.
They would stay.
My poems.

Without fear.
In private intimacy.

I'd kill those people.

Scriptures say, murder is a great act.
Lies.
Sounds like truth, doesn't it?

Special

Then they named me a special child.
They think I'm special.
A 'speciality' baby. Mother cries. I laugh. Baba[83] is on the terrace. Watering plants, tears.
Ma thought she'd die by suicide. Baba thought of remarrying.
A new flower will bloom. Phuchka[84] every evening. Reading compound word spellings from adarshalipi[85] books on taal[86]-leaf.

I can talk. But I won't. My khala[87]'s harmonium. Let them open up the reeds. I'll make a bicycle. I'll ride it. On a road free from traffic I'll ride rains. I'll ride sunshine. Will ride breeze. Will ride boats.

Ma thought. I'll draw. Baba. I'll write. Uncle. I'll sing. Brother. I'll tear apart.
I tear apart.
Time.
Politics.

SABERA TABASSUM (b. 1978)

Bird

(For sculptor Novera Ahmed)
Who wants the heart of a bird
all people want is bird meat
some want the seamless wings to fly
some the boon of sharp bird gaze—
a black cat's paw can turn
the bird into cold meat
even then she loves both the bird and the cat.
Grains for the bird
and meat for the cat
she has to go to opposite kind of shops.
Still she loves cat and bird
one for the other
one against the other
she keeps them as pets…
till the time the bird blurts out its last chirp
till the time the cat licks blood off its paws.
The bird's heart—a tiny globe—
lies in the cold room for five days.
A rose on one shoulder
the other bearing the dead bird
she shuts down the basket lid
once the lid shuts the feet are done with all their work

the two hands at last are free.
Then in the garden burns 'A Snake Named Desire'[88].
The garden then sees
a fantastic coffin fly up on raptured wings!

My Heart Walks with You

Hell and I are two spilt fruits
stones in pocket, a river un-split
in the rain-splash of dead sparrow's eyes
my heart walks with you

Once you appeared in the drinks
songs of desire that the intoxicated mind sings

Wish once in the field of sacred congregation
my heart walks with you

A life expansive as the question asked
in only hand's touch is distance marked
intellect's stairwell gets eaten by a heaven of bugs
my heart walks with you!

ASMA BEETHE (b. 1980)

Coin

A tiny round brownish metal coin
hundred years of history on both sides
travelled far and wide and changed many hands
passed around by both the thief and sage
crossing seas, borders, the earth's lines
where will it stop on which extended palms
its rolling days see some wager and debts
lament-wishes for the dark-round sphere

Archaeology has dug up its kingdom
the script erased from the king's blurry face
The remnant of bones inside the earth know
There are tears stuck to the erosive copper coin.

Door

Rusted since long; the termite-chewing
hum keeps my ear busy. On both sides two
cursed songs of the earth. Once it stops
this city seems a distant planet. Faraway
din and noise like the crickets' buzz…
Once that stops I feel the familiar
wooden door—it doesn't stay lifeless
its decay plays on with the termite's song

Six seasons stand unwinking, motionless
the plastic paint covering the bright darkness
tells me: nailed inside, there's a tune of
forever waiting, an unshakable silence.

Celebration

Let's get on the train ticketless
today we'll break the discipline of violin
we'll fly away as far as our eyes go
if we feel like then a few days in a village
we'll stay back, sure, we'll not return
we'll not think pros and cons, our ties lie,
where, how? We'll go, will leave behind the way
a train's metallic grind leaves everything behind
hold hands firm before the charm wears off
love crumbles down under burden of rights
in the path where silent winds blow
we will go, I know we all finally go
the night is waning, come let's go out
to catch the first train of the cloudy dawn of doubt

NITU PURNA (b. 1981)

Matriarchy

Every day in the moon light, one bird—errs once
and breaks its wings, voice of one woman on one moonlit night
one song in high note—is it tragedy or wounded pride!

More evenings, nightlight more haplessness of sleep
more daring more impatient limits of celebration, mid-river and a rocking boat
human sanctuary after all stories are told—the strong pull of shelters…

The way the night time wind picks up force once a house caves in

> sun rays turn newer;
> the girl thinks each day
> the girl cries every day
> the girl sees each day the body of the unbeauteous
> the girl forgets each day the pain of being mute
> the girl wakes every day in her sleep
> the girl loves every day
> the girl searches every day
> the girl only moulds herself each day …

Dead Logs on the Bed

The weight of placid age calls at blood to be out in the streets
in the left bank the call of the river is like a charm
                boishakh[89] sweat sets the chest afire.

The sweat-stricken placid body calls at the mind
restless feet break the inner calm.

Within the restless night glows a faint light
dead logs lie on the bed waiting to become coal

Oh in my grandfather's home
random chirping by birds of the forest—
old stones rubbing against each other;
restless fires must appear just like this.

When the burden of placid age calls upon the restless blood
even before it turns to coal
                does a foolish fire rage aflame!

ASMA ODHORA (b. 1981)

Recurrent Verse-Spheres

Sharp pointed stars do not emit moonlight,
only the moon can; gazing away ...

The evening star changes to Pole Star at dawn,
and Toynbee Circular Road is all washed out,
this recurrent time, how suffocating it is!

My unresponsive speechless unpublished poems
on the disinterested nightly footpath;
they crane their necks in the alleyways to search for the verse-spheres of dark!
The night walks by the drains, keeps hollering in its deep voice.
And the quiet moonlight sleeps with hands
folded under its head on the wide main road!
On the railing of an over-bridge!

See how the waning night tries to grope the moon with its blackened hands
it robs the middle class grace of the fountains—
a separation ensues with the unresponsive stars.

Jibanbabu's[90] stars knew to die;
Jibanbabu's stars knew to die ...

I put my Pole Star to sleep

at the start of a light about to emit
still I'll let the love live between the moon and my Pole Star
let there be some light, at any rate—
in the darkness that even erodes the sea!

I Open Flowers, the Shape of Errors

The watermark on my lap and cheeks is hidden by the palm of my closed fist. Then like a paper boat of my childhood I turn my mind into a drongo's tail, snatch all the errors from this bright golden hue of the afternoon which is the mirage of light. The moment I blow off all the repressed grey-coloured emptiness, the blue sky stretched from corner to corner of the horizon peers through the peep-holes of my chest. Oh my companion from across many births! Do you know what colour are the dead stars left to float on keya[91] leaves?

The evening that approaches making way through a narrow alleyway, its folds know—koels[92] die the moment fireflies stop flying along longitudes, constellations cover their face in pitch black muslin, and from within the eroding wound sprouts the lotus of corrosion. Laugh, O, horizon; keep laughing!

The solitude-loving cancer laughs out, all of these bright sunlight and afternoon know, how a light violet colour hovering over the fragrance of lemon blossoms strongly pulls at existence. But violet itself means stain and scorch; then in shame the veiled photon hides their face in the red of the krishnachuda blooms.

Come jingling anklets
Come cloud-messenger
Come shower-sounds
Come closer enchanting water forms...

AFROJA SHOMA (b. 1984)

Scarecrow

Now that so many springs are gone it seems
she was standing alone
in the midst of a helpless noon
spreading out hands like a scarecrow.

One spring bird in her chest
had cooed in deep secrecy
the sweet tremor broke her apart
moment by moment, defenceless

After many spring are gone she sees
like Arjun[93]'s arrow
one sharp spring
has pierced her down, left her without remedy.

The Days of Camping

In the days of camping in thick winter—
falling dew drops seeped through tents the whole night;
the music that dripping mist makes—
we have realised this in solitude.

Mingled in the dove's cry
we have set on our chests
each noon
like pendants
before we die;

Our chests are sea shells
they lie open on the pages of the diary;

Still the days of camping stay alive in our hearts
we realize, to go closer to the ultimate
without any expectations, this heart
like muslin it should be spread out in the path of the mist.

Dawn

Let the cruel path be over;
show us the doorway.
Even while the world calms down at night;
let there be dawn for
the bird that cries.
The Earth like a mother
she has laid bare her love
for the souls of enemies and friends.

Let love spring in the heart of the enemy;

Let there be dawn for
those that cry through nights.

RIMJHIM AHMED (b. 1985)

Sound

I return homewards, breaking off the breeze from your soiled sari.
Although we don't have our own house in this life. Perhaps we won't, even in the next birth.
I think all this while I bite my nails, maybe nail my teeth! My tunic stained with the prophecy.
All unmindful-ness I rub on my palms.
The day wanes on the path of bird flights. The dusk-sheathed village looks on—
how humans keep spinning in the sphere of life.
Their chest nothing but a wide and empty kabaddi[94]-field.
Lying sprawled on the soft shawl of winter is our Victory Day[95]. The green and red all torn up.
With dusk-light falling deep I feel within me a house, a courtyard, I feel like a home.
A fever dense on my forehead descends like the colour of white mist.
Dust gathers in the creases of my age. My masked face still retains its own expression.
Only this noise I hear—
your statue being hammered down in the next room.

Distance

Where do afternoons of neem-flowers roll off,
the fields of kabaddi sport?

Eyebrows change gestures.

In which tremulous nerve does vibrate the brass flute

Soulful bhairavi[96].

The lost dust of fields, sunny shades of sandalwood
dogs running. Fireflies burning in the leaf of imminent dusk

So many paddy bugs come swarming in the crops here!
They see an invisible secret on the visible screen. Sold to leaf-wrapped earth sky

Alone on the way, a lonely way.

You come off from my body like an ancient decrepit structure.

They

I hang my frankness, my ware for sale
at times they come to buy words
they do not pay any dime or money
offer a smokescreen, a cover of disguise

Even they've understood, I get sold for nothing

There's amrit in venom, and with that thought
I drink in gulps a sea full of bitter poison

They come—buy words—they leave
mud from the shoes sticks to the doormat

No one stays back.

SHAFINUR SHAFIN (*b.* 1987)

Sickness: 2

I sense how it is that all over my body keeps growing
a city, mythical roads with glass marbles in their pocket,
a pine sprig standing stunned, someone's cry!
Beyond a rusted iron gate,
from a lobbed-afar childhood
one can hear the tuneful play cries of children:
"At the fair, here we play, see that lonely girl who sighs,
She's got no friend, get up girl, wipe those tears from your eyes!"

Like sleep, a bath is most intimate an act to humans.
Suddenly pushing the bathroom door ajar
the half-mad woman's direct poison gaze!

Tunes melt into the thin air. Childhood evaporates!

One day a madman ran with a live chicken in his hand
towards an eatery at the street corner, dropping the bird in the burning wok.
I can sense, even when a man goes mad his subconscious knows,
meat ought to be cooked! I can sense a pair of murderous red eyes
rushing towards me—I close my eyes!

Inside my sleep I hear disobedience—
everything crashing down… once I sleep I get lost.

In my sleep the loud wail of the mad siren of the asylum.

All sicknesses assemble prone on the Juhu Beach balconies, slowly ringing laughter, madness melting in the thin air, slowly …

Black Swan

The word 'door' in the dictionary is a strange one
the moment you open it there's the call to enter—
as soon as it closes, beyond it
the interior décor,
the faces of masks in a row,
piled feathers
in the Kathakali [97] body of dancer
stuck to the wall,
the scene of tearing off these feathers
by her own hands.

Oblivious of dance gestures
the stairs have descended
towards the path of scattered feathers

MAHI FLORA (b. 1987)

Travel Stories

*

The foolish girl breaks the flute, tears off leaves
after loving intensely she discards easy conversation to a far-off machine.
Does the afternoon ever tell itself all the travel stories?
The leaves burn from old envy, dry straw in dirty meal plates,
old scores to settle at the chin,
finger's tap at the beauty spot, lightly all day long like first love!

**

At the last moment
the very last local passenger bus
won't go anywhere today,
that's how a downcast heart decrees.
It starts to rain like a human chain.
Everything soaked wet.

***

Dry coconut shells like hollow skull pieces,
lying all over the city, loveless;
the way after ardent lovemaking
all that remains is easy affection.

Grape Vine

I've been brought over here by the boy's kite flying from across
the garden. There's a river. Also there's waiting.
That boat from brave waters have ferried me here!
Happiness of the mirror. Walking paths through parted hair, the
home yard.
Fragrant cilantro leaves green chillies on warm rice!
Hand-mixed rice with water of the netherworld.
I've been placed here by the boy's secret sense of hurt.

Farms full of blooming flax flowers. A desperate hunger countrywide.
Childhood is in the grip of winter, decay.
I'm holding the hands of self-interest.
I've been left here by the boy's unbridled love!
The strings caught in the web of poush[98].
I've been left here alone.
Sight, smell, indolent time rolled into crying.
I'm hugged by astringent clouds! The boy's mind.
A victorious blue star. The dark of the night!
How long am I held captive, how many days, moments, hours such
as these!

Grape vine twined around my fingers!
Freedom, come hug me all over!
Freedom, come hug me all over!

SHWETA SHATABDI ESH (*b.* 1992)

The Chill in Our House

We didn't have any ice making machine
yet there was a twelve-month long winter in our house—
from warming our hands in fire
the fate line of the palm is singed, now illusory!
Thinking spring will arrive, I'd sprinkle
rain every morning in the garden of wind.
All over the body of the red-oleander
are envelopes of illness filled with leaves!
Growing up this way we thought
winter was just absolutely natural—
all other seasons being wrong pronouns.
Who knows where all residents left and went far away,
I was the first to find springtime
here in your company among all.
This isolated breeze riddled with nerves of time
I couldn't like springtime for too long!
The melody of return to the bosom of mist-shadows,
in the depth of our home
songs are congealed of winter's chill and cold!

Alahiya

After murdering himself Alahiya[99] had shattered all mirrors
of the world—
I don't know him, but while thinking of him
distance seems easy.

Alahiya had said, "The eyes of the world is red!"
Fists open up feeling the pain of hills crashing down
So, tying his eyes in red banners
one day he himself gets murdered—trapped in his own sensibility!

Alahiya, who we never knew well!

Still, like an old letter
he keeps hiding inside the folds of eyelashes.
And whenever I tell a story about him I remember,
how a tired stricken flower had fallen withered
the way dusk comes enveloping before a green evening!

Poets' Bios

1. **Sufia Kamal** (1911-1999): Born in Barisal and a teacher at the Calcutta Corporation School in undivided India, she had received blessings and admiration from the two Bengali literary icons: Rabindranath Tagore and Kazi Nazrul Islam. After the partition of the subcontinent, she relocated to the then East Pakistan, eventually becoming the undisputed spokesperson and leader of the women's rights movement. She published collections of poems, prose, autobiography, travelogue, etc. She was awarded Bangladesh's all major civilian awards including the Bangla Academy Prize for poetry.

2. **Khaleda Edib Chowdhury** (1937-2008): Poet, novelist and essayist, she was born in Cumilla and studied Bengali literature in Dhaka University. She worked as journalist and teacher for some time before joining Bangladesh government's Information Service. She published more than 40 books including several volumes of poetry. She was awarded the country's highest literary award, the Bangla Academy Prize in 1993.

3. **Anwara Syed Haq** (*b.* 1940): Poet, fiction writer, and feminist, she was born in Jessore, and later went on to study medicine in Dhaka Medical College. She trained as a Clinical Psychologist, and subsequently did her post-graduate studies in London, UK.

Parallel to her professional commitments, she continued writing across different literary genres, and published more than 80 books of poetry and prose. Life partner of Syed Shamsul Haq, one of the doyens of contemporary Bengali literature, she was awarded the prestigious national literary award, the Bangla Academy Prize.

4. **Farida Majid** (1942-2021): Bilingual poet, translator and academic, she was born in Kolkata, India, and moved to the then East Pakistan after the Partition. She went to London, UK, for higher studies and got involved with the liberation movement of Bangladesh in 1971. She translated major Bangladeshi poets in English and recited them during the demonstrations to garner support for her people. She set up an independent press named Salamander Imprint and published from it subsequently. Later, she moved to the US, studied Comparative Literature at NYU, and also taught Bengali at Columbia University and English at CUNY. Author of one collection of Bengali poetry published in 2016, Farida Majid died of cancer in September 2021.

5. **Meherun Nesa** (1942-1971): A working class, self-taught poet, she was born in Kolkata, India, and moved to the then East Pakistan after the Partition in 1947. Faced with tremendous hardship due to the forced migration, she had to undertake various menial jobs to support her family. An active participant of the Bengali nationalist movement, Meherun Nesa took up writing as a tool of protest. She was brutally murdered by the local cohorts of the marauding Pakistani military force during the early days of the military

crackdown. A collection of her complete poems was published posthumously.

6. **Zeenat Ara Rafiq** (1944-2005): Born in Kolkata, India, she moved to the then East Pakistan after the Partition in 1947. She studied Bengali literature in Dhaka University and embraced teaching as her profession. Wife of Mohammad Rafiq, another prominent poet of Bangladesh, she wrote poetry from an early age, but published only a couple of poetry collections during her lifetime. She had also been a passionate singer.

7. **Suraiya Khanum** (1944-2006): Born in Jessore, she studied English literature in Karachi University, Pakistan, and later at Cambridge, UK. After completing her Master's degree, she returned to Bangladesh and joined Dhaka University as a faculty member. She quickly became involved with the intelligentsia and Dhaka literati, and published her first poetry collection *Nacher Shabda* in 1976. She later moved to the US to pursue her PhD at Arizona State University where she taught subsequently. She died as a recluse in the US in 2006.

8. **Rubi Rahman** (*b*. 1946): Born in Kolkata, India, she moved to the then East Pakistan after the Partition in 1947. She studied English literature in Dhaka University and pursued teaching as her profession. A progressive cultural activist, she was also a selected female member of the country's National Parliament. She published three collections of poetry and was awarded the coveted literary

award, the Bangla Academy Prize. Rubi Rahman was an invited participant at the prestigious International Writing Program of the University of Iowa, US, in 2008.

9. **Kazi Rozi** (*b.* 1949): Born in Khulna, she studied Bengali literature in Dhaka University. She joined the country's liberation war in 1971 as a clandestine radio artist and later became a member of the National Parliament. Primarily a poet, she also wrote fiction, essays, etc., and published around 20 books. A cancer survivor and a tireless social activist, she was awarded the country's top literary award, the Bangla Academy Prize.

10. **Zarina Akhter** (*b.* 1951): Poet and educationist, her first book of poetry came out in the year 1986. She is the author of four other poetry collections including one anthology of flash poems. She has written a book of literary essays too. She was a teacher and head of the department of Bengali language and literature of a renowned women's college before retirement.

11. **Nasreen Naim** (*b.* 1952): Poet, fiction writer and essayist, she studied Bengali language and literature in Dhaka University. She later chose teaching as a profession, and have recently retired as the principal of a reputed high school in Dhaka. She has more than 20 books to her credit.

12. **Shamim Azad** (*b.* 1952): Bangladeshi-born British bilingual poet, storyteller and writer currently based in London, UK. She has

published 37 books of poetry, fiction, essay, play, autobiography, etc. She attended the world-famous Edinburgh Fringe Festival in 2012 presenting her poetry and storytelling. She was the 'poet in residence' in 'A Poet's Agora', Athens, in 2019. She is also a recipient of 'The Artist in the Community' award, London.

13. **Dilara Hafiz** (*b.* 1955): Poet, researcher and educationist, she studied Bengali literature in Dhaka University and obtained her PhD degree. She taught all her life before retiring as Chairperson of the Dhaka Education board. Wife of the renowned poet Rafique Azad, she has nine books of poetry and a few collections of essays. Her poems were translated into English by the American poet and researcher Caroline Wright.

14. **Anjana Saha** (*b.* 1955): Originally from the southern part of Bangladesh, presently she is settled in Dhaka. A self-taught poet, she has published 14 books of poetry. Apart from being a prolific poet she is also a passionate singer of Tagore songs. Her husband Asim Saha is also a veteran poet and publisher of Bangladesh.

15. **Nurunnahar Shirin** (*b.* 1956): Originally from Cumilla, she spent a substantial part of her creative life in Chittagong and is presently settled in Dhaka. She studied Bengali literature and subsequently wrote for the country's major literary supplements and magazines extensively. Reclusive and introvert in nature, Shirin has published 14 books of poetry and a collection of literary essays.

16. **Nasima Sultana** (1957-1997): A harbinger of new voice and poetic diction of women's poetry in modern Bangladesh, she studied Bengali literature in Rajshahi University. Later she settled in Dhaka, working for various newspapers and magazines. Before her untimely death due to cancer, she published three books while her complete poems were published posthumously. Many of her poems were translated into English and are included in the anthology *Majestic Nights: Love Poems of the Bengali Women* (2008) edited by the American poet Caroline Wright.

17. **Shahjadi Anzuman Ara** (*b.* 1958): One of the very few women of post-liberation Bangladesh who embraced modern poetry as a vehicle of their creative expression. She has written extensively for literary magazines and published four books of poetry. She obtained a Bachelor and a Master's degree from the University of Dhaka. Shahjadi was a member of the administrative service of Bangladesh Government and an Additional Secretary before retiring recently.

18. **Jharna Rahman** (*b.* 1959): A multifaceted writer, poet, novelist, short story writer, playwright, essayist, editor, and writer of children's literature. She has written around 60 books including eight collections of poetry. Until last year she taught Bengali literature in an esteemed college of Dhaka. A passionate singer and cultural activist, she runs a literary organization named Parankatha and edits a journal by the same name.

19. **Taslima Nasrin** (*b.* 1962): Poet, prose writer, physician, and feminist, she was born in Mymensingh, worked in Dhaka, and was eventually forced out of the country in 1994 for a prolonged period of exile in Europe, USA and India, due to her strong views on women's rights and criticism of religious bigotry. She has authored more than 40 books including several poetry collections, and a seven-volume series of candid autobiography. Many of her works are translated in English and other major languages, and have received numerous awards. She was awarded the prestigious Sakharov Prize, Simone De Beauvoir Prize, and Ananda Puraskar, India, among others. Currently, she is based in New Delhi, India.

20. **Rahima Akhter Kalpana** (*b.* 1962): Poet, researcher, editor, and lyricist, she is currently one of the directors of the prestigious national institution, Bangla Academy, Dhaka. She has authored 28 books in diverse fields of literature, out of which 12 are poetry collections. She also specializes in writing haiku and currently serves as the Secretary General of Bangladesh Haiku Society.

21. **Ferdous Nahar** (*b.* 1962): Poet, essayist and lyricist, she was born and brought up in Dhaka, where she did her post-graduate studies in Dhaka University. She has published 15 poetry collections and three books of essays. An avid traveller, she loves to draw during leisure time. She is presently based in Toronto, Canada, and is working on her first book of poems in English translation.

22. **Bilora Chowdhury** (*b.* 1966): One of the proponents and practitioners of the new modern Bengali poetry of the eighties, she was a student of Dhaka University. Bilora contributed regularly to the leading literary magazines of Dhaka and Kolkata, India, before migrating to and settling in Singapore. Since then, she is not that visible in Bengali literary scene but nevertheless continues to be regarded as a powerful poetic voice.

23. **Shahnaz Nasreen** (*b.* 1967): Poet, novelist, and short story writer, she was born in Cumilla. She has a Master's degree in Economics from University of Chittagong. She has four poetry collections, three short story books, and two novels. She runs a literary organization named Poetry Platform with two fellow female poets. A senior government employee, Shahnaz is also a documentary film maker.

24. **Kochi Reza** (*b.* 1968): Predominantly a poet, she was born and educated in Bangladesh, where she worked in the judiciary department but moved to the US subsequently. A prolific author, she has authored more than 15 books of poetry. Apart from these, she has two short story collections. She is the editor of a literary magazine and is now based in California, US.

25. **Leesa Gazi** (*b.* 1969): Initially known as Leesa Autondrila, she was born in Chittagong and later moved to Dhaka. Eventually, she migrated to the UK and started writing in English under the name of Leesa Gazi. She is the founder director of the Komola

Collective, an active theatrical organization. She was the co-writer and performer of the theatre production *Birangona: Women of War* which was later turned into an award-winning documentary film titled *Rising Silence*. Recently, she has resumed writing in Bengali and published her debut novel named *Rourob* which was translated into English, titled *Hellfire* (Westland Books, India, 2020). Leesa is currently working on her first feature film based on one of her own short stories.

26. **Shahnaz Munni** (*b*. 1969): Poet, novelist, short story writer and essayist, she also writes for children and the young adult. She has a Master's degree in Sociology from University of Dhaka. She has been writing for last 30 years and has 24 books to her credit, including a few poetry collections. Shahnaz Munni is a television journalist and currently heads the news department of a reputed TV channel.

27. **Shelly Naz** (*b*. 1969): Born in Sylhet, she studied Zoology in University of Chittagong and currently works for the Social Welfare Ministry of the government of Bangladesh. She has published nine books of poetry. Women's subjugation and the phenomenon of the male domination in Bangladeshi society are the core concerns of her poetry. She is currently pursuing her Ph.D. degree in Women and Gender Studies in Australia.

28. **Nahar Monica** (*b*. 1969): Poet, short story writer, and novelist, she was born and raised in Rangpur, a northern district of Bangladesh.

She has a Sociology degree from University of Dhaka, and a Master's degree in Health Policy, Planning and Financing from University of London, UK. She has six books to her name including a poetry collection. Monica lives in Montreal, Canada, with her family and works for the Health Department of Quebec province.

29. **Aysa Jhorna** (*b.* 1969): Poet, translator and teacher of English literature in Dhaka, she has 11 books to her credit including six collections of poems. She has translated *Ariel* of Sylvia Plath, poems of C. P. Cavafy, and compiled a collection of leading women poets of the world translated into Bengali. Her own poems have also been translated and published in various reputed international literary magazines.

30. **Shanta Maria** (*b.* 1970): Poet, essayist and journalist from Dhaka, she has 11 books to her credit including five collections of poems. After working as a print and electronic media journalist for several years, she worked with China Radio International in Beijing in 2011-2012, and is currently teaching Bengali language at Yunnan Minzu University, China.

31. **Megh Aditi** (*b.* 1970): Poet and fiction writer hailing from the northern part of Bangladesh, she has done her post-graduate studies in the department of Public Administration of Dhaka University. She has seven books of poems and short stories. She also runs a literary organization named Oihik Bangladesh and edits a literary journal by the same name.

32. **Monika Chakraborty** (*b*. 1971): A graduate from Dhaka University, she writes both fiction and poetry, and has published eight books. Her only poetry book titled *Aparthiba Gan* is a bilingual one. She is also a professional singer, enlisted for radio and television performance.

33. **Alaka Nandita** (*b*. 1971): Primarily a poet, she was born and educated in Chittagong where she studied Bengali literature in University of Chittagong. Later she moved to Dhaka and attended the Young Writers Project at Bangla Academy. She has three poetry collections along with a book of biography. After her stint as a freelance journalist for some time, she became a development professional and is currently employed with a reputed NGO of Bangladesh.

34. **Farhana Rahman** (*b*. 1972): Poet and film reviewer, she was born and raised in Dhaka, where she studied English literature at Eden College. She has three poetry collections and a book of short stories. An ardent cinema aficionado, Farhana's film reviews have been collected in a book. After working as a teacher for a few years, she joined an international organization, and is currently looking after her family business.

35. **Junan Nashit** (*b*. 1973): Dhaka-based poet, essayist, fiction, and children's literature writer, she has published 15 books including six collections of poems. She studied Economics and chose journalism as her profession. Junan Nashit worked for several daily

newspapers and a television news channel for a few years before joining the Government News Agency of Bangladesh, where she is a senior journalist at present.

36. **Nahida Ashrafi** (*b.* 1973): Dhaka-based dynamic poet, fiction writer, editor and publisher, she has published five collections of poems including a bilingual one titled *Tenets of Sadness*. She runs a publishing house named Jaladhi and edits an eponymous literary journal too. She is the founding director of a thriving literary space called Poetry Café in Dhaka. She has received numerous literary awards at home and abroad.

37. **Audity Falguni** (*b.* 1974): Poet, short story writer, translator, researcher, and essayist, she was born in Jessore. A graduate from the Faculty of Law, Dhaka University, she worked for number of newspapers, publishing houses, and national and international development agencies including the UN. She has so far authored more than 30 books including four collections of poems, short stories, translations, children's book, essays, etc., and won several literary awards.

38. **Rahima Afrooz Munni** (*b.* 1974): Poet, novelist, and short story writer, she has a Master's degree in Islamic History from the Eden College, Dhaka. She is the author of four poetry books and a novel. She has recently finished making her first full-length film titled *Chashma* based on her own story.

39. **Jahanara Perveen** (*b*. 1975): Poet and essayist, she is the author of six poetry books. She has also written two books of literary prose on poets T. S. Eliot and Rainer Maria Rilke. An acclaimed journalist who has worked for many reputed print and electronic media, she currently works for the popular news channel Independent TV.

40. **Novera Hossain** (*b*. 1975): Poet, novelist, and short story writer, she has a Master's degree in Anthropology from Jahangirnagar University, Dhaka. She is the author of six poetry books, two short story collections, and a novella. A teacher and researcher for several years, now she is a full-time writer. She has recently edited the Collected Poems of a brilliant young poet named Shameem Kabir who died by suicide a few years ago.

41. **Shakira Parvin** (*b*. 1977): Dhaka-based poet, she originally hails from the southern part of Bangladesh. She has two Master's degrees, one in Theatre Studies and another in Film and Media. She has published eight collections of poems, a bilingual poetry collection named *Fallen Neem Flower* (2019), and another collection in English translation titled *Amour* (2019). She currently teaches Film Studies in a private university.

42. **Sabera Tabassum** (*b*. 1978): With a degree in Anthropology from Jahangirnagar University, Dhaka, she worked in the development sector for many years before becoming a full-time writer. She has published 14 collections of poems including one book of translation of the famous Indian poet and lyricist Gulzar. She is

currently engaged in translating the well-known American poet Sharon Olds.

43. **Asma Beethe** (*b.* 1980): Born in Chandpur but grew up in the port city of Chittagong where she studied at University of Chittagong. She is primarily a poet, but has a growing interest in photography and documentary filmmaking. A journalist by profession, she is currently employed with a leading local newspaper. She has published four collections of poems, and also edited a literary journal named Ghuri.

44. **Nitu Purna** (*b.* 1981): Born and brought up in Narayanganj, Dhaka, she is primarily a poet who was also the first female literary editor of a national newspaper of Bangladesh. She has authored four collections of poetry. Later she migrated to Canada, trained as a professional social worker, and is now employed with the mental health department of the government of Alberta province.

45. **Asma Odhora** (*b.* 1981): Born and brought up in Dhaka where she studied English Literature. She is primarily a poet but also an editor, entrepreneur, and publisher. Author of three collections of poetry, she is also a dynamic social activist working for the empowerment of women and wellbeing of children. Asma is an avid traveller and trekker.

46. **Afroja Shoma** (*b.* 1984): Born in Kishoreganj, she studied in Dhaka University obtaining her Master's degree from the

department of Mass Communication and Journalism. She is the author of five collections of poetry. She also writes journalistic prose, fiction, and essays. Afroja is an Assistant Professor at the American International University, Bangladesh. Simultaneously, she freelances with BBC Bengali service.

47. **Rimjhim Ahmed** (*b*. 1985): Born and brought up in Chittagong, she studied Sociology and also has a degree in Law. A talented and promising poet, she is the author of three collections of poetry, and has recently published a highly acclaimed novel titled *Bismoychinher Mato*. Rimjhim is currently working in the development sector of Bangladesh.

48. **Shafinur Shafin** (*b*. 1987): Poet and translator, she was born and raised in Chittagong. She studied English Literature in Chittagong University, and South Asian Studies in Kashmir University, India. She is the author of a poetry collection named *Nissangam* and a collection of English translations of shorter poems of Imtiaz Mahmud, titled *Gandamphul*. Currently, she teaches at a private university, and edits the poetry section of an online journal named Prachya Review.

49. **Mahi Flora** (*b*. 1987): Born and raised in Rajshahi, she is a teacher at Government Model School and College of Rajshahi Board of Education. A prolific poet of unique style and diction, Mahi Flora has already published six collections of poems.

50. **Shweta Shatabdi Esh** (*b*. 1992): The youngest poet of this anthology, she has already gained much reputation for her unique poetic voice, style, and subject matter. She was born in Jamalpur district, and studied Bengali literature in Dhaka University. A prolific poet, Shweta has published five collections of poems. She has received two awards, one from Bangladesh, and the other from India, for one of her recent books Beeparit Durbine.

Curator's Bio

ALAM KHORSHED (b.1960), graduated as a Mechanical Engineer from Bangladesh University of Engineering and Technology, Dhaka and did his Post Graduate studies at Baruch College of City University of New York, USA. He worked for, among others, GlaxoSmithKline Pharmaceuticals in Chittagong, and Canadian Aviation Electronics (CAE) in Montreal, Canada. He eventually returned to Bangladesh in 2004 to embrace his real passion: arts and literature. He is now engaged as a full-time writer, translator, critic and arts organizer. After successfully running a unique socio-cultural organization named 'Bishaud Bangla' in Chittagong for nine years, he founded a new arts space called 'Bistaar: Chittagong Arts Complex' in December 2014, and has been working as its Founding Director since. He has authored more than twenty books in Bengali, mostly works of translation and literary essays. Among them, the most notables are: translations of Virginia Woolf's *A Room of One's Own*; *Reflections*, an autobiographical book of Henry Miller; an anthology of poems of the Polish Nobel laureate Wislawa Szymborska; a book length conversation between the two great Argentine writers Jorge Louis Borges and Victoria Ocampo translated from the Spanish; *The Jaguar Smile*, the first work of non-fiction by Salman Rushdie, and *I Shall Marry When I Want*, a Play by the Kenyan writer Ngũgĩ wa Thiong'o.

Translator's Bio

NABINA DAS is the author of five books. Her poetry collections are *Sanskarnama* (Red River, 2017), *Into the Migrant City* (Writers Workshop, 2013), and *Blue Vessel* (Les Editions du Zaporogue, 2012). Her debut book is a novel titled *Footprints in the Bajra* (Cedar Books, 2010), and her short fiction volume is titled *The House of Twining Roses: Stories of the Mapped and the Unmapped* (LiFi Publications, 2014). A Rutgers-Camden MFA alumna, Nabina is the editor of *WITNESS, poetry of Dissent* (Red River, 2021), and co-editor of *40 under 40, an Anthology of Post-globalisation Poetry* (Poetrywala, 2016). Nabina's poems appear in Poetry (Poetry Foundation), Prairie Schooner, Indian Literature (National Academy of Letters), Caravan, Poetry at Sangam, The IndianQuarterly, Economic and Political Weekly, Dhaka Tribune, The Yellow Nib Anthology (Queens University, Belfast), and Six Seasons Review, among several others. Nabina is a 2017 Sahapedia-UNESCO fellow, a 2012 Charles Wallace Creative Writing alumna (Stirling University, Scotland), and a 2016 Commonwealth Writers features correspondent. Nabina has worked most recently as a teaching faculty, a journalist for 10 years, and also as media executive in NGOs and industry bodies like the CII (Confederation of Indian Industries), in the area of Gender, Development, Child Welfare, and Environment. She writes columns and commentaries for several newspapers and journals. Born and brought up in Guwahati, Assam, she is also a 2012 Sangam House, a 2011 NYS Summer Writers Institute, and a 2007 Wesleyan Writers Conference creative writing alumna. Nabina's new poetry collection *Anima and the Narrative Limits* will appear in 2022 from Yoda Press.

Glossary

1. kajal—dark kohl adornment used for eyes
2. Muktisena—liberation forces of Bangladesh who fought against the Pakistani forces
3. aanchal—part of the sari that is draped around the upper body or head
4. zari—gold thread work of embroidery used on saris or other attire
5. shiuli—also shefali/parijat; night-flowering jasmine
6. mallika—chrysanthemum
7. Kajla Didi—name of a young girl from the renowned Bengali poem "Kajla Didi" by Jatindramohan Bagchi; a character with tragic traits whose absence/death is grieved by the narrator/poet
8. shaal—also sal; shorea robusta, used as timber for housing, etc.
9. shimul—silk-cotton tree; bombax ceiba
10. krishnachuda—also gulmohar or peacock flower
11. jarul—myrtle; a deciduous tree with bright pink or light purple flowers
12. sheetal-paati—woven mats made from 'murta' (Schumannianthus dichotomus) plants, surface has a cool feel quality, hence termed sheetal (cooling)
13. Gorky—the name given to the deadliest storm and tidal wave of 1970 that killed nearly five million people of the then East Pakistan
14. ayat—a verse from the Holy Quran of varying lengths that make up the chapters (surah) in the holy book
15. Qayyum—Qayyum Chowdhury, a first generation painter and artist from Bangladesh

16 Mahakaal—literally means 'beyond time or death'; a deity common to Hinduism and Tantric Buddhism
17 Glasnost—a term popularised in the mid-1980s by Mikhail Gorbachev as a political slogan for increased transparency in Soviet Union
18 paanch-foron—a whole spice mix of five (paanch) items used in Bengali cooking
19 Kanai—a nick name of Krishna, the cowherd god
20 kaash—a perennial grass whose fleecy white flower blooms during autumn
21 Mahalaya—the beginning of "Devi-paksha" (end of the mourning period for ancestors), and said to be the day Goddess Durga had killed the demon
22 Age of Ignorance—(Arabic: جَاهِلِيَّة, romanized: jāhilīyah, lit. 'ignorance') is an Islamic concept referring to the period of time and state of affairs in Arabia before the advent of Islam in 610 CE. The term jahiliyyah is derived from the verbal root jahala "to be ignorant or stupid, to act stupidly"
23 amrit—nectar of eternal life or youth in mythology, literally means 'immortality'
24 Ahalya—wife of Sage Gautama who was cursed to turn into a stone until Rama, prince of Ayodhya, liberated her back to her human form
25 moksha—a concept common in Hinduism, Buddhism, Jainism, Sikhism, etc., to indicate enlightenment, emancipation, liberation, and release from one's human life
26 Ekalavya—a character from the epic Mahabharata, of the forest dwelling nishada (hunter) tribe; his teacher Drona asked him to sacrifice his thumb as fee and obeisance to his Guru, which is seen as a move to deter Ekalavya from becoming the superior archer over Drona's favourite student Arjuna
27 jaba—hibiscus
28 bokul—also bakul; evergreen tree with fragrant flowers

29 Peacock Throne—the legendary jewelled throne that was the seat of the emperors of the Mughal Empire, later plundered and seized by Nadir Shah
30 belphool—jasmine
31 ilish—Hilsa fish
32 jui—jasmine
33 Kalpurush—Orion constellation
34 Draupadi—the heroine of the epic Mahabharata, wife of the five Pandavas
35 Dushshashan—the younger brother of Duryodhan, the Kaurava chief and adversary to the Pandavas
36 chandan—sandalwood
37 azaan—the Islamic call to prayer delivered by a muezzin at prescribed times of the day
38 antara—in Hindustani classical music it is the second part of a composition usually sung in higher notes
39 matryoshka—Russian stacking dolls that are placed one inside of the other in decreasing sizes
40 neem—Indian lilac, bearing bitter leaves and barks having medicinal qualities
41 abhaya—a concept common to Buddhism, Jainism, and other religions signifying fearlessness, mercy, or compassion
42 Brindaban—also Vrindavan; a town near Mathura, Uttar Pradesh, India, famed as a place where Krishna performed his divine activities
43 Quo vadis—a Latin phrase meaning 'Which way are you marching/going?'
44 orna—stole, veil, or scarf worn over a shirt or tunic by women in South Asia, often covering the head and chest, to observe modesty as per social norms
45 kali—also kali yuga or the era of darkness, vice, and misery
46 sitar—a string instrument used in Hindustani classical music for playing ragas

47 ashadh—the first month of monsoon season, and the third month in the Bengali calendar
48 apsara—beautiful female spirits mentioned in Hindu and Buddhist cultural texts, depicted in South Asian dance, sculpture, and literature
49 udaara, mudaara, taar saptak—base octave, middle octave, and high octave in the seven notes used for ragas in Hindustani classical music
50 aaheli—pure, perfect
51 Ishaan—the northeastern corner of a plot or structure in ancient vastu shashtra (texts on architecture and design), said to be auspicious
52 shankha-sindoor—white conch shells made into bangles, and red vermillion powder that most Hindu women wear as signs of marital status
53 kaashphul—same as kaash; white fleecy grass flowers blooming in autumn
54 Devi—Mother Goddess in Hindu, Buddhist scriptures
55 ahimsa—nonviolence, a concept specific to Hinduism, Buddhism, Jainism, etc.
56 hoor—or houri; beautiful women—often said to be a separate creation other than human females on earth—that accompany faithful believers in Paradise, according to Islamic religious belief
57 tamasha—spectacle, incident, often employed in derogatory or mocking sense
58 sharaab—alcohol
59 jamdaani—an artistic weave in cotton saris with figures or flowers, known worldwide as a special craft from Bangladesh
60 haritaki—Indian Hog Plum, a plant with medicinal fruits
61 jhaaptaal—A 2-3-2-3 pattern in 10 beats used in raga expositions in Hindustani classical music
62 shava-sadhana—a tantric rite where the practitioner sits on a dead body to conquer mortal feelings of fear or attachment

63 arhar—Pigeon Peas; a yellow coloured-lentil used in South Asian cooking
64 sanyas—renunciation of worldly ties and possessions by Hindu mendicants
65 kojagori—ko+jagori means 'who stays awake'; refers to the full moon night of the autumn worship of Lakshmi, the goddess of wealth and peace, when people are supposed to stay awake throughout the night to see Lakshmi enter their homes
66 krosh—an ancient unit for measuring distance in Bengali, 3,000 meters or 1.8 miles
67 Altamira—a prehistoric cave art site in Cantabria, Spain
68 Israfil—the angel in Islamic tradition who blows the trumpet to announce the Day of Judgement
69 chaal—rice; move, as in chess; roof cover of corrugated tin sheets or bamboo, and mannerisms of a person
70 beli—jasmine flower
71 gondhoraj—Gardenia flower
72 hasnahana—Lady of the Night flower
73 esraaj—a string instrument often used in classical raga traditions
74 hemanta—late autumn, the season preceding winter with cooler temperature
75 Dol—Holi is also known as Dol in Bengal
76 Holi/Hori—the festival of colours celebrated in spring
77 Kanhaiya—a nick name of Krishna, the cowherd god
78 Braja gopis—women of Braja who played Holi with Krishna
79 bisarjan—also visarjan; immersion, referring to idols of Hindu deities being submerged in water after ritual worship is over
80 srabon—also sravan, the monsoon season of rains
81 dadi—paternal grandmother
82 sindoor—vermillion, red powder applied by married Hindu women on hair parting and forehead
83 Baba—father
84 phuchka—a snack made from fried puffed dough, had with condiments

85 adarshalipi—alphabets manual, usually a prescribed text for children
86 taal—palm tree/leaf
87 khala—maternal aunt
88 Title of a famous sculpture by Novera Ahmed
89 boishakh—also baisakh/vaisakh, the first month of the summer season and beginning of the Bengali calendar
90 Reference to Bengali modern poet Jibanananda Das (1899-1954)
91 keya—Screwpine flowering plant with long leaves
92 koel—Asian cuckoo
93 Arjun—the third of the five Pandava brothers in the epic Mahabharata
94 kabaddi—the national sport of Bangladesh, a team game
95 Victory Day—also Bijoy Dibosh, the national holiday of Bangladesh celebrated on Dec 16 to commemorate the victory of liberation forces of Bangladesh over Pakistani forces in 1971
96 bhairavi—a raga in the Hindustani classical music tradition, a morning raga
97 Kathakali—a traditional dance drama form from Kerala, India, with elaborate facial makeup and varied gestures
98 poush—early winter, the ninth month in the Bengali calendar
99 Alahiya—a male name

www.ingramcontent.com/pod-product-compliance
Lightning Source LLC
Chambersburg PA
CBHW021437080526
44588CB00009B/570